Jesus, You're Fired!

How Evangelicals Traded the Kingdom of Heaven for an Earthly Empire

STEPHEN H. PROVOST

Dragon Crown Books 2020
All rights reserved.

ISBN-13: 978-1-949971-17-0

Dedication

To all those who have ever been inspired by the words of Jesus to seek something better within.

"Those who can make you believe absurdities can make you commit atrocities."

Voltaire,
French philosopher

Contents

1 Personal Journey 3

2 Jesus People 11

3 New Dominion 21

4 Miracles for Sale 33

5 Evangelical Ties 45

6 Blowing Bubbles 57

7 Lighting the Fuse 69

8 Abortion Distortions 91

9 Messianic Mindset 105

10 Donald and Bathsheba 129

11 Activating Prejudice 151

12 Lost Causes 165

13 Hearing is Believing 183

14 Martyr Don 215

15 The House Always Wins 225

16 Out with a Whimper 239

17 The End... 247

Jesus, You're Fired!

How Evangelicals Traded the Kingdom of Heaven for an Earthly Empire

"It's very hard for a democracy to function if we're operating on just completely different sets of facts."

Barack Obama,
44th president of the United States

Personal Journey

I spent more than a decade in the evangelical church in my teens and early twenties. Although I eventually left for a variety of reasons, I remember that period of my life fondly.

I was sixteen when I was introduced to Christianity, the child of parents who didn't attend church and didn't bring up the subject of religion apart from a perfunctory, yet sincere prayer around the dinner table at the holidays.

My mother was a positive-thinker who took

comfort in an inspirational magazine called *The Daily Word*, my father a former Methodist who came, later in life, to describe himself as a "hopeful agnostic."

The church provided me with a safe place to explore the meaning of life, insulated from the kind of peer pressure that demanded I "get high," party and fit in with the crowd — a crowd that doled out acceptance based on little more than surface conformity.

The church seemed to me like a better fit.

I was attracted by the teachings of Jesus, especially the idea that a "kingdom of heaven" was "at hand" — accessible to anyone, and that the spirit of God could be found within.

As a teenager who'd been bullied in childhood, I was encouraged by Jesus' references to the meek inheriting the earth and "the least of these" being worthy of kindness.

I went in with my eyes open, saying to myself, "I don't know if this will work for me, but I'll give it a try. What do I have to lose?"

I didn't know at the time I'd be subjected to a different kind of peer pressure that made me equally uncomfortable, but that came later, as I learned more about the church — and as the church itself began to change during the 1980s.

I had philosophical questions no one seemed to want to answer; at least, they didn't want to do much more than quote scripture and encourage me to "have faith."

I didn't want to feel pressured into "witnessing" any more than I'd wanted to feel pressured into partying. Hadn't Jesus urged his followers to pray in private, not in public to gain attention? He'd told them to lead by example: "You will know them by their fruits."

I also didn't like feeling pressured to donate a certain amount of my income. (As a teenager, I didn't have that much in the first place). I didn't understand how followers of a man who had declared "you cannot serve both God and money" could put such an emphasis on tithing — an Old Testament law that had supposedly been superseded by Jesus' new covenant of grace.

Even Paul had said that giving wasn't a matter of law, but choice: "Each one must give as he has decided in his own heart, not reluctantly or under compulsion, for God loves a cheerful giver."

It seemed to me that, if the church needed money to support its programs, it should just say so. But it didn't work like that. Guilt trips and paradoxical appeals to selfishness (the more you give, the more God will reward you) worked better, so that's what they did. As I saw televangelists asking for money to support their lavish lifestyles, I began to understand that these were people who worshipped at the altar of capitalism and ignored Jesus' declarations about the poor being blessed, because "theirs is the Kingdom of Heaven."

They weren't the least bit interested in the Kingdom of Heaven. That wasn't their goal; if anything, it was an obstacle. Their objective wasn't heavenly truth or spiritual enlightenment.

It was an earthly empire built not on the teachings of Jesus, but on the twin pillars of money and power.

"And no wonder, for Satan himself masquerades as an angel of light."

It can be a convincing disguise.

STEPHEN H. PROVOST

"Why should the devil have all
the good music?"

Larry Norman,
Christian musician and songwriter

STEPHEN H. PROVOST

Jesus People

I didn't know it at the time, but when I was first exposed to Christianity in the late 1970s, it was in the midst of a civil war.

The form of Christianity I embraced was already losing.

It had grown out of the 1960s hippie movement, both as an aspect of it and a reaction to it. The Jesus People, as they called themselves, wore their hair long, and preferred home Bible studies to church services. They talked about Jesus a lot, but because they *wanted to*, not because they felt they *had to*. They even had their own brand of rock 'n' roll music, made by people like Larry Norman, whose long blond hair made him look every bit the part of the typical flower child.

Except he wasn't.

He talked to the hippies in their language, but instead of talking about free love, he warned about the dangers of "gonorrhea on Valentine's Day" for people who were "still looking for the perfect lay." To Norman, the hippie movement was asking the right questions, but coming up empty. His message: "Why don't you look into Jesus? He's got the answers."

Norman had gotten his start with a group called People!, who'd had a hit with a song called "I Love You" but parted ways with Norman over his Christian message.

But that didn't mean he'd found (or sought) acceptance in the mainstream church, either. Many traditional Christians viewed him as a wolf in sheep's clothing.

Yes, Norman was singing against casual sex and the use of drugs ("shoot junk till you're half insane, a broken needle in your purple vein"), but he was still playing rock 'n' roll. And they were convinced that was "the devil's music."

His first album was "too religious for the rock and roll stores and too rock and roll for the religious stores." And subsequent releases (with the exception of the blockbuster Bible bookstore hit *Only Visiting This Planet*) were similarly caught between two audiences.

Secular musicians, meanwhile, were finding an audience with Jesus music, which created further scorn and distrust among the hymn-singing crowd.

Jesus Christ Superstar magnified the Christian generation gap. And when DJs started playing pop-Christian tunes like "Jesus is Just Alright," and "Spirit in the Sky" alongside Zeppelin and Deep Purple, it just proved the critics' point: Jesus Music was mimicking the ways of the world and could not be trusted.

But to Norman and others, the opposite was true: If you didn't speak the language of hippies and street people, they'd never hear the message of Jesus. In fact, that's what Jesus himself had done.

"I want to encourage other people to try to discover who they are, not to try to fit into some superficial prototype of what they think a Christian should be, but to discover who they really are," he said. "That's what I try to encourage people to do, to become the complete person that Christ has made them."

This, of course, was at odds with the cookie-cutter, toe-the-line demands of church leaders who preferred their own "superficial prototype" to an honest, self-aware Christianity.

Backlash

It wasn't the first time that a different, more personal form of Christianity had arisen to challenge a dogmatic status quo. The Protestant

Reformation had emerged as a reaction to the oppressive, top-down dominance of the Catholic Church in the Middle Ages. And, it could be argued, Jesus' own movement was a response to the legalism of the Pharisees and the Herodian puppet government installed by Rome.

Each movement offered direct access to the divine — a "priesthood of all believers" that bypassed clerical power brokers who profited as middlemen between God (as they imagined him) and the faithful. And, to a greater or lesser extent, the rebels prevailed.

But in each case, their victory proved to be fleeting, as a new class of leaders inevitably rose up to wrest power back from the people. This has often happened in the secular world, with autocrats moving in fill the void in the chaotic aftermath of popular uprisings. (The French and Russian Revolutions, are examples, as is the overthrow of the Soviet Union. In Cuba, the revolutionaries themselves became autocrats.) And it's been no less true within Christianity.

The Jesus Movement proved to be among the most ephemeral of these movements, with Norman claiming the mantle as the "Father of Christian Rock" but being largely marginalized after the 1970s.

Norman's blunt lyrics and street-level focus put him in the crossfire of the Christian civil war: denied secular acceptance for his outspoken pro-Jesus message and shunned by the mainstream church as a rebel trying to rocking the boat.

Middle-aged pew-sitters accustomed to hearing the same, canned sermons each Sunday felt threatened by anything that sounded different, and in the end, they won the day. As the hippie culture faded into the 1970s, the Jesus Movement tried to evolve into something else, but it didn't know what that "something" should look like. In the end, it wound up looking a lot like the old establishment. Bible studies like The Vineyard outgrew their home-church digs and moved into permanent buildings, while older churches made modest concessions as they absorbed the aging Jesus People.

The former "holy hippies" cut their hair and turned down the music. They migrated to growing suburban megachurches, which accepted their more casual speech and demeanor as long as they ditched the rebellious attitude of the late 1960s and early '70s. More contemporary music was tolerated, at least in some quarters, as long as it came in a glossy, non-threatening package.

The Jesus Movement was gradually absorbed or shoved aside by a corporate brand of Christianity that better reflected the Reagan era. Indeed, Ronald Reagan's embrace of evangelical megachurches sealed the fate of the "personal gospel" that had briefly challenged the status quo.

It was this unholy alliance between evangelical conservatives and the Republican Party that set the stage for an unstated rejection of Jesus' Kingdom of Heaven in exchange for an earthly empire. Power-hungry Christians had their foot in the door, and they were about to force it wide open.

"Compel them to come in."

Augustine (quoting Jesus),
bishop of Hippo

STEPHEN H. PROVOST

New Dominion

It may seem ironic that the 1980s saw both the ascendance of a new kind of Christianity and a new focus on self. But it's only ironic if you think of Christianity in terms of a moral or ethical system.

Despite the name "Moral Majority," the group founded by Jerry Falwell in 1979 was neither. It wasn't even focused on morality, but power. The organization's main objective was to transform evangelical Christianity into a political force.

And it accomplished that goal.

In a 2006 poll by the Pew Research Center nearly two-thirds of white evangelicals approved of their leaders actively expressing their political views. That compared with less than half of Catholics and mainline Protestants.

The invisible wall separating church and state — one of the nation's most basic principles — was crumbling, at least among this group of voters. And it's a significant group: According to Pew, evangelicals (3 in 4 of whom are white) make up more than a quarter of all Americans, more than any other religious group. Catholics rank second at a little more than 20%.

Evangelicals account for more than half the population of Tennessee, and nearly half the residents of Alabama (49%), Arkansas (46%), Kentucky (49%), and Oklahoma (47%). That's a huge bloc of voters, and their power is magnified by the fact that they vote overwhelmingly for one party: Republicans.

In exchange for their support, Republicans

shifted their own goals to meet evangelical priorities. On the surface, this meant embracing evangelical stands on hot-button issues like abortion, homophobia (disguised as "religious freedom"), gun rights, and prayer in public schools.

But these issues, as important as they've been to true believers, were always a means to an end for some in the evangelical movement: replacing democracy with a theocracy. Breaking down the separation between church and state was the first step to casting off democracy in favor of a government by the Christian God — as defined by their leaders, of course.

There's even a name for it: Dominionism. The term is based on the mandate in Genesis for Adam and Eve to claim "dominion" over the earth and everything in it. It's a verse that's been used to justify everything from mistreating animals (who, contrary to *All Dogs Go to Heaven*, aren't believed to have souls) to polluting the environment. It's also convenient justification for Republicans who value fossil fuels and business savings above any impact on the environment.

But these ideas, too, are just a means to an end for Dominionists. Not many of them will come right out and *say* they want to undermine democracy, but if they're pressed, they'll say they'd prefer the rule of God to a government of the people, by the people, for the people.

So, within the context of democracy, they've supported people who promote "Christian values" — which really has very little to do with values and is, instead, code for promoting Christian rule.

City of God

The alliance with Reagan was the first tentative step in this direction, followed in 1988 with televangelist Pat Robertson's campaign for president. Robertson became famous for saying natural disasters were God's punishment for the nation's acceptance of homosexuality. According to Robertson's logic, they were God's way of nullifying the rule of the people — who had voted for and practiced acceptance — by *force.*

That's an important point. Dominionists don't frown upon imposing their will on others. In fact, it can be their preferred way of doing things, justified in their minds by a single line from one of Jesus' parables:

"Compel them to come in."

These words are found in Jesus' parable of the great banquet, the story of a host who invites a number of people to a celebration — and is chagrined when they tell him they can't attend. Insulted but determined, he then instructs his servant to go out and invite all the "poor, the crippled, the blind, and the lame." But even after they accept his invitation, there's still room at the table, so the exasperated host sends his servant out to "go out to the roads and country lanes and *compel them to come in*" (emphasis mine).

There it is. If people won't accept Jesus,

they can be compelled to do so. Augustine, the early 5th century bishop of Hippo in North Africa, seized upon the verse to justify Christianizing the Roman Empire and forcibly subjugating its citizens to the will of the church. In contrast to the Kingdom of Heaven, Augustine focused on the concept of establishing an earthly kingdom in subject to the church.

For Augustine, the end justified the means. In a letter to a fellow church official, he explained that the use of force had been instrumental in bringing a group called the Donatists to heel.

The Donatists didn't think priests who had renounced their faith under threat of torture should be allowed to administer church sacraments unless they were baptized and ordained again. Augustine disagreed.

Originally, he thought that "no one should be coerced into the unity of Christ" and that the church should make its case "only by words" and trust that it would "prevail by force of reason."

But he changed his mind after realizing that

reason wouldn't work with some people, simply because they were too deeply rooted in their family traditions. He wondered how many people only remained in the Donatist heresy "because they had been born in it, and no one was compelling them to forsake it and pass over into the Catholic Church."

In short, if they didn't join the church voluntarily, forcing them to do so was fine and dandy. Translated into the modern era: If democracy doesn't support the evangelical agenda, it's acceptable to pursue a different approach.

An autocratic approach.

Evangelicals had grown impatient in waiting for the Second Coming, a time when "every knee should bow" and "that every tongue should confess that Jesus Christ is Lord."

In the early late 1960s and early '70s, an Orthodox Presbyterian minister named R.J. Rushdoony proposed returning to a medieval theocratic model based on the laws of Moses. His neo-feudal Calvinist concept rejected the values of the Enlightenment and devalued rational thought.

In fact, he suggested humanity's ability to reason had been tainted by the fall of man. The only true reason came directly from God, via the Bible, which must therefore form the basis of any sound government.

Since all sound laws were based on the Old Testament commandments anyway, why not go the whole distance and adopt them as the basis for government? Literally. Adultery, idolatry, homosexuality, witchcraft, blasphemy, and other crimes would all carry the death sentence. And democracy itself should be abolished, because it placed the will of man above the will of God.

Christianity and democracy were "inevitably enemies," and in fact, democratic systems were a form of heresy.

This view that the Old Testament law was the basis for *all* valid law led Roy Moore — when he was chief justice of the Alabama Supreme

Court — to install a 2.5-ton granite monument of the Ten Commandments in front of the state courthouse in 2001.

By that time, the push to "restore" America's status as a "Christian nation" had gained momentum thanks to high-profile televangelists such as Jerry Falwell, Pat Robertson, James Dobson, and others. Their methods and views may have varied, but they all shared this goal to a greater or lesser extent.

Falwell proved to be a seminal voice. He rejected Rushdoony's attempt to replace democracy with theocracy. Instead, Falwell saw democracy as a tool to be used in restoring Christianity as the nation's dominant force.

He believed the majority — a moral majority — of Americans agreed with him, and he formed the Moral Majority in 1979 to support this idea, seeking to break down the wall of separation between religion and politics.

On the surface, he seemed to be calling for Christians to become involved in democracy by making their voices heard, but his ultimate goal had less to do with democracy than a "higher calling": the establishment of a Christian kingdom on Earth, just as Augustine had done and Rushdoony had suggested.

There was always a duty to God and country, but never a doubt that God came first — and it was best if there was no contradiction between the two. The more they could be brought into alignment, the better.

For men with this goal, the implied answer to Jesus' rhetorical question the always the same:

"What will it profit a man if he gains the whole world, yet forfeits his soul?"

The answer was, "Quite a lot."

Power was the goal.

And profit, indeed, was the cornerstone of their motives.

"Give, give, give expecting to receive, so you can give, give, give!"

Kenneth Copeland,
televangelist, *Giving and Receiving,* 2014

STEPHEN H. PROVOST

Miracles for Sale

For more than a millennium after the age of Augustine, the Catholic Church ruled Europe with an iron fist. It became the sole arbiter of truth, keeping the subjects of its earthly kingdom in their place (and lining its coffers in the process) with a simple two-step approach to repression.

Step One was the threat of force. Heresy would not be tolerated. If you didn't affirm the church's teachings, you would pay the price — with your property, your freedom, or sometimes your life. It didn't matter how absurd those teachings were (that Earth was a few thousand years old or that it was at the center of the solar system): You couldn't question them.

If you even knew about them, that is, because Step Two of the church's strategy was to control the flow of information. Masses were said in Latin, a language most of the faithful didn't understand. It furthered the idea that priests were both a privileged class and gatekeepers for the truth. Most congregants were illiterate, anyway, and relied on the church to interpret the Bible for them.

This was important because the Bible and church teachings were considered the only valid sources of truth. If anything contradicted, or even seemed to contradict them, well (to borrow a phrase), God help you.

Flash forward to the evangelical message of today. There's one difference: Bible reading is encouraged. But the scriptures are still interpreted by the church leaders and funneled through "approved" channels — such as the pulpit, but by other means, too. The rise of televangelism gave conservative churches another means of reaching their audience, and of persuading them to tune out everything else. Secular news, music, and entertainment were "of the world" or "of the devil," and should be shunned. Science was viewed with suspicion, because it didn't always agree with the church's teachings. Case in point: Evolution. Genesis stated that the world had been created in six days. The flood was another problem: There was no geological evidence for it, and no indication there had ever been that much water in the atmosphere.

If science was wrong about these things, it could be wrong about other things, too. For some, it was better to "expect a miracle" than to see a doctor, because God could be trusted — and science couldn't.

This was the end result of Augustine's repudiation of reason, and it played into the hands of church leaders who wanted their flocks to rely solely on God (or their self-serving vision of him).

They became purveyors of miracles and healings, hawking them — or the promise of them — in exchange for "pledges." In other words, money. Catholics had promoted similar practices in the Middle Ages, selling "indulgences" from Rome that amounted to "get out of purgatory free" cards. The more money you gave the church, the less punishment you had to endure in the afterlife. It had been a major criticism of Protestant reformers, who didn't believe in purgatory and viewed the practice as corrupt.

By the 1980s, however, a new generation of Protestants was taking a page out of the old Catholic playbook. They held crusades where evangelists would "lay hands on" people from the audience who said they were sick. These people would then fall backward into the arms of a waiting assistant, "slain in the spirit," and rise to declare themselves as good as new.

The practice has been criticized by skeptics such as James Randi, who made it his business to expose frauds, ranging from faith healers to self-described psychics. Randi, a musician himself, focused on con artists who used parlor tricks and the power of suggestion to fool their audiences.

In a 1986 appearance on *The Tonight Show* with Johnny Carson, Randi revealed that an evangelist named Paul Popoff used an earpiece to eavesdrop on backstage interviews his wife conducted with audience members before they came forward to seek healing. When they did, Popoff appeared to know things about them he couldn't have possibly known, unless it had been revealed by the spirit.

That specific practice was later lampooned by Chevy Chase in a scene from the 1989 film *Fletch Lives*, and fellow *Saturday Night Live* veteran Steve Martin played a faith healer three years later in *Leap of Faith*.

People who were supposedly healed at the

events were encouraged to show their appreciation by gifts of cash, even though many experienced nothing more powerful than the placebo effect.

But it didn't stop there.

Televised crusades served as infomercials for the power of God, as transmitted through the hands of the televangelist. If you couldn't make it to one of the crusades — and most viewers couldn't — you could call up and pledge a few dollars in exchange for the evangelist's intercessory prayer.

Serving Mammon

The traveling big-tent revivals had always had something in common with old-fashioned medicine wagons. Now, television fused the itinerant preacher and snake-oil salesmen seamlessly into a con game built for the late 20th century.

You could also buy everything from Bibles

to videos. You could pick up a cross necklace or a framed print of Jesus for your mantel. You could enroll in a mail-order (or, later online) course. Or, of course, you could just give outright to support the ministry. The more the better.

Where did the money go?

Evangelist Ken Ham built a $101 million re-creation of Noah's Ark to promote the flood story... and make money off visitors. Jim and Tammy Faye Baker opened a theme park called Heritage USA that drew 6 million visitors a year. Oral Roberts and Jerry Falwell founded Christian universities in Oklahoma and Virginia, respectively.

Kenneth Copeland, Pat Robertson, Benny Hinn, Jimmy Swaggart, and Joel Osteen became multimillionaires, with their sermons broadcast into living rooms nationwide and around the globe.

Copeland was, perhaps fittingly, the richest of the bunch, with his net worth reaching more

than three-quarters of a billion dollars by 2020:
Fittingly, because he's been perhaps the foremost
proponent of the prosperity gospel, embodied in
the slogan "name it and claim it."

The prosperity gospel is a combination of
wishful thinking and transactional theology. The
transaction in question typically involves a gift to
the evangelist's ministry, which is portrayed as an
expression of faith. The promised (though
seldom delivered) reward for this faith is
prosperity far beyond the amount you've
donated.

Predictably, this system feeds on some of the
poorest viewers: They are, of course, the most
desperate for a miraculous windfall. But the
transaction is a con. There's no guarantee that
anyone will get rich off it — except, of course,
the evangelist. It's like buying a lottery ticket
from an unscrupulous merchant who guarantees
it will be a winner.

The new evangelicals knew that building
their own wealth depended on keeping those

who believed them desperate, so they'd keep giving, just like gamblers who keep pulling the handle on a slot machine, convinced that the next attempt will yield a jackpot.

It's a method based on a simple principle called the dopamine effect. Dopamine is a chemical in the brain that makes you feel good. But its levels don't rise when you experience pleasure, as you might expect: They grow based on the *expectation* of a reward. So, as long as your expectations are high, you feel good. If, however, you don't get the reward you're expecting, you're in for a letdown.

The trick, then, is to keep you in a state of perpetual expectation. That's where the concept of faith comes in.

Evangelical Christians are encouraged to "have faith" regardless of the results. In fact, seeing results nullifies faith. To support this process, evangelicals seize on scriptures such as the definition of faith found in Hebrews, where it's described as "the assurance of things hoped for, the conviction of things not seen."

But since faith is the cornerstone of evangelical Christianity, the hoped-for reward is implicitly *something to be avoided*. This is an astonishing idea, but it keeps the faithful in their place by perpetuating the dopamine effect. The ultimate reward can't even be achieved in this world, but only after death. Then believers will enter the kingdom of heaven — transformed from a spiritual state "within" to a place adorned with pearl gates and streets of gold. It's the ultimate in wealth and prosperity.

Visions of sugar plums to keep the dopamine flowing.

"Why should I apologize because God throws in crystal chandeliers, mahogany floors, and the best construction in the world?"

Jim Bakker,
televangelist

STEPHEN H. PROVOST

Evangelical Ties

When Ronald Reagan finished his second term, evangelicals found themselves without a champion. Reagan had been great, but he was more an ally than one of them, and they couldn't help but wonder what it would be like to have one of their own in the White House.

Enter Pat Robertson, a Southern Baptist minister who founded TV's Christian Broadcasting Network in 1960. The network was supported by its flagship news and devotional show, *The 700 Club* — named for 700 viewers who pledged $10 a month to keep it running.

CBN spawned a spinoff of sorts called *The PTL Club* (which stood for either "Praise the Lord" or "People that Love"). Jim Bakker, an Assemblies of God minister, became host of *The 700 Club* in 1966 and continued in that role for eight years before venturing out on his own wife Tammy Faye to found PTL.

The split was probably a good thing for Robertson, who was able to maintain his reputation while Bakker became embroiled in a series of scandals. Among them: a $279,000 payoff to a church secretary to cover up a sexual encounter at a motel, which she alleged was a rape (Bakker admitted the encounter but denied the rape charge).

Bakker resigned from PTL in 1987, but that wasn't worst of it. He'd embraced a prosperity gospel message and begun spending lavishly, with detractors referring to PTL as "Pass the Loot." Two years later, he was convicted on 24 counts of mail fraud and wound up serving time in prison.

He would return to television after his release, though less visibly. More on that later. But it was in the 1980s that Bakker and his first wife — whose heavy makeup led Time magazine to label her "televangelism's dolled-up super-shopper — became poster children for the excesses and abuses of televangelism.

In 1988, the same year charges were brought against Bakker, fellow televangelist Jimmy Swaggart became embroiled in a sex scandal of his own. He tearfully confessed in a televised "I have sinned" speech, and was removed from the pulpit by the Assemblies of God.

Entering the Fray

None of this stopped the continued rise of the evangelical movement, as a scandal-free Robertson announced a bid to succeed Reagan as president. Robertson's father had been a U.S. senator, and more than most other evangelists, he had focused his telecasts on political issues: speaking out against gay rights and abortion, while advocating for prayer in public schools.

If anyone doubted Robertson was for real as a political force, he put those doubts to rest in the Iowa Republican caucuses, the first electoral contest of the presidential race in a conservative Midwest state that was tailor-made for the Christian broadcaster.

He shocked everyone by finishing second in Iowa, behind Bob Dole but ahead of the sitting vice president, George H.W. Bush. Ultimately, he was unable to build on that momentum, finishing fifth in the follow-up New Hampshire primary: a disappointing effort that doomed his candidacy.

Despite this, other politicians with ties to the evangelical movement followed in his footsteps. Pat Buchanan, a Catholic who shared many of the movement's values, ran for president several times and attracted a substantial following.

Mike Huckabee, a Baptist pastor who served as a staffer for televangelist James Robison, entered politics and served as governor of Arkansas from 1996 to 2007. His tenure served as a springboard for a presidential campaign in 2008, where Huckabee found success in Iowa just as Robertson had — actually going him one better by winning the caucuses.

His strong showing demonstrated that evangelicals were gaining influence within the GOP, and he went on to win seven primaries and caucuses before dropping out of the race. The old-line party establishment remained in control, but Huckabee's strong showing may have helped persuade nominee John McCain to select Alaska Gov. Sarah Palin — an evangelical favorite — as his running mate.

Barack Obama would later suggest that Palin's nomination served as a springboard for Donald Trump's ascendancy. Whether or not there's a direct correlation, one thing is undeniable: Even more than during the Reagan era, the party was becoming dependent on its ties to conservative Christianity.

In five straight presidential contests, starting in 2004, evangelicals voted overwhelmingly for Republican candidates in the general election. As this was occurring, however, the GOP as a whole was struggling. By 2020, its standard-bearer had won the popular vote just once in the previous eight presidential elections. Leaders kept trying to expand the party's appeal by pushing for a "bigger tent," but nothing seemed to be working.

What Golden Rule?

As the party writ large was losing ground, white evangelicals were growing more committed to it, which only magnified their growing clout in the shrinking tent. To use a popular metaphor, they were the biggest fish in a smaller pond.

And they were growing.

The time was ripe for them to consolidate power, and they did so with the help of a new movement called the Tea Party. Founded in 2009 as an anti-tax, small-government movement, it gradually became a platform for evangelicals to promote their social platform.

The more the GOP relied on white evangelicals, the more starkly it came to reflect their values. In the process, objectives that had been concealed for decades beneath a cloak of "civility" began to resurface.

Evangelicals became emboldened by their burgeoning status within the GOP bubble to speak out more plainly. They used the First Amendment to justify this new blunt language by condemning the "censorship" of political correctness.

The upshot: The Golden Rule was out, and rudeness was in.

Might meant right.

And money meant power.

A conservative Supreme Court had already affirmed the use of wealth as a weapon by striking down limits on campaign spending — ruling, in effect, that spending money on elections was a form of free speech. This decision, *Citizens United v. FEC*, bound evangelicals (especially those who had embraced the gospel of prosperity) even more closely to the fiscal conservatives of the Republican Party.

These conservatives had long been working to accumulate and concentrate wealth in their own hands while both exploiting low-wage workers and blaming them for their plight. The result: welfare reform of the mid-1990s, and, later, a concerted assault on the Affordable Care Act.

Corporations were finding ways to avoid paying for medical insurance by employing more part-time workers. They were ending pensions, decimating unions, and fighting any attempts to raise the minimum wage. In doing so, they were concentrating wealth and power in the hands of shareholders — at the expense of workers.

Employees now had to work two or three jobs just to make ends meet. And Republicans sold them on the idea of fighting for the "good old days" of low-wage, hazardous jobs in coal mines and steel plants rather than pursuing safer, higher-paying jobs in the sectors like the tech industry.

No wonder the party found common cause with evangelical leaders, who had been using the prosperity gospel as an excuse to bilk millions of dollars out of desperate low-income supporters for decades. It's often forgotten that the pursuit of wealth cuts both ways: Not only does it line the pockets of the rich, it keeps the poor "in their place" and prevents them from challenging those in control.

The status quo must be preserved, and if it appears to have been weakened, it must be restored to its former glory.

By making America great again.

STEPHEN H. PROVOST

"People almost invariably arrive at their beliefs not on the basis of proof but on the basis of what they find attractive."

Blaise Pascal,
French intellectual, *De l'art de persuader*

Blowing Bubbles

Evangelical leaders were strengthening their
bond with corporate America and, in the process,
their hold over the Republican Party — aided and
abetted by their own burgeoning media empire.

Like the Catholic Church in the Middle
Ages, they systematically began to isolate their
supporters by cutting them off from secular
media: "fake news" which was "of the devil."

In doing so, they created their own
alternate reality of false facts that were, to
objective observers, just as absurd as the old

Catholic assertions such as the idea that the sun revolved around the Earth (which furthered the self-centered notion that humanity was literally at the center of the universe.)

From the 1950s through the 1970s, free television had shattered the Christian bubble by bringing objective journalism into American living rooms every night. Newspapers, once party mouthpieces, had become more independent during this period, and the mainstream media were serving as both gatekeeper and watchdog. They thwarted the anti-Communist propaganda of Joseph McCarthy, exposed the abuses of the Vietnam War, and brought down a president by uncovering the "dirty tricks" of Watergate.

Baby boomers who grew up during this period thought of this media model as the norm. Everyone watched Walter Cronkite or Huntley and Brinkley, and almost everyone accepted that they were telling the truth.

But at the end of the 1970s, something

happened to change that: the advent of cable television. Cable was originally set up to provide clear signals to rural areas that were beyond the reach of static-free UHF and VHF broadcasters. (Remember rabbit ears?) But in short order, cable operators were operating original programming — and charging for it.

As this occurred, the media began to fragment, with new outlets emerging that catered to various tastes. First came specialty channels dedicated to sports, movies, and news, etc. Then new, more targeted and competing outlets emerged.

This specialization wasn't new. Radio had been doing it for decades, with formatted programming for country music, Top 40, hard rock, and, notably, news. In the late 1980s, radio paved the way for further specialization in this latter category with the debut of Rush Limbaugh's conservative talk radio program.

Limbaugh presented the news through a conservative lens, offering an alternative to the mainstream media — which had long been distrusted on the right as too liberal. Limbaugh's program became the most popular thing on radio, and it served as a template for things to come. Imitators were quick to jump on the bandwagon, and soon, talk radio became a haven for conservatives. They stopped watching the nightly news and listened to Limbaugh's "take" instead. Before long, they were tuning in to a whole different world populated by right-wing pundits like Michael Medved, conservative lifestyle guru Laura Schlessinger and paranormal conspiracy theorist Art Bell.

It was an alternate reality that became not just an escape, but a place where conservatives came to spend most of their time.

Fox in the Henhouse

Of course, it was only a matter of time before the concept came to cable television, which had been dominated to that point by Ted

Turner's Cable News Network (CNN). Initially, however, it took a more muted form than Limbaugh's radio bombast.

Fox News touted itself as a "fair and balanced" alternative to the more liberal CNN, and from a conservative perspective, it was exactly that. News shows were complemented by conservative pundits such as Bill O'Reilly — who touted himself as an independent voice despite clear leanings to the right. In doing so, he gave conservatives permission to believe their ideas weren't out of step, after all.

Sean Hannity, who would become the network's biggest star (and by far cable's highest-paid host) came over from CNN. There, he had co-hosted a show with Alan Combs, who provided a liberal counterpoint to Hannity's conservative voice. CNN had pioneered this debate format with *Crossfire*, a show that featured Tom Braden "on the left" and Pat Buchanan "on the right."

What Fox News did was remove the left

side of the equation and let conservative pundits loose to voice their opinions unchecked.

Like-minded viewers loved it, and tuned into Fox in droves as they abandoned CNN — which soon fell behind in the ratings. Fox had hit the motherlode, striking the same vein Limbaugh had on radio and, more to interestingly, using the same method televangelists had employed in the 1980s: preaching to the choir.

O'Reilly, Hannity, and their fellow Fox commentators became the equivalent of political televangelists, spreading the gospel of conservatism to an audience eager to tune out everything else.

The more that audience stayed in this bubble (which Fox encouraged them to do so it could maximize its ratings) the more conservative ideas reinforced themselves as they talked to one another... on the internet.

As influential as Limbaugh and Fox were, it was the internet that really severed conservative and evangelical thought from the rest of the world, creating an echo chamber where the ideas spread by Limbaugh, Hannity, and others could be repeated and reinforced.

The more people hang out exclusively with those who agree with them, the more extreme their views tend to become. They feel safer espousing radical ideas and speaking out in terms that might be condemned in the broader world. Churches had used this method to reinforce their dogma for centuries, by providing not just spiritual fulfillment, but a social structure to go with it.

When evangelical churches embraced political activism in the '80s, they encouraged members to rely on them exclusively for social interaction. Secular outlets ranging from fraternal organizations to rock concerts were condemned as tools of the devil that should be avoided. After all, you didn't want to expose yourself to temptation.

In the new millennium, conservative chat rooms, websites, and Facebook pages became extensions of this social bubble. And as visitors to these sites shared both evangelical and politically conservative ideas, those two concepts became even more fully integrated.

They also became more extreme, amplifying other similarities, such as racial and cultural in-group biases. Within groups of largely white, rural American voters, views that reinforced that identity were magnified, as were views that condemned those who didn't fit the "proper description." If you lived in a city, held liberal views, were the wrong color, or the wrong sexual orientation, you were persona non grata.

These ideas fed upon themselves in isolation. If the bubble wasn't "pure" enough, its members would leave and form a new bubble all their own. They'd leave Fox News for One America News or Newsmax, and they'd ditch their Twitter accounts for the more Trump-friendly Parler.

But things became combustible long before

OAN or Parler came on the scene. Aggrieved evangelicals, nationalists, and others were gathering fuel for their fire even before Trump himself came along.

All that was left was something to provide the spark that would ignite a wildfire. As it turned out, that something was some*one* — and it wasn't Trump. It was a Black American senator from Illinois named Barack Obama.

STEPHEN H. PROVOST

"It was as if my very presence
in the White House had
created a deep-seated panic."

Barack Obama,
44th president of the United States

Lighting the Fuse

When Barack Hussein Obama was elected president in 2008, many saw it as the culmination of a dream. It was a sign that the United States had finally achieved the kind of equality to which it had long aspired. Yes, there was still work to be done, but Obama's election was a signature milestone. Not only had a Black man been elected president, he had defeated a popular, respected war hero (John McCain) — in a landslide.

Clearly, the era of intolerance and bigotry was coming to an end. More evidence came when

Obama was re-elected in 2012, again defeating a well-respected, principled opponent in Mitt Romney.

Three years later, in 2015, the Supreme Court ruled that the Fourteenth Amendment required all states to allow and recognize same-sex marriages: more evidence that the world was changing.

That same year, a billionaire real estate developer-turned-reality TV star named Donald Trump announced what most people thought was a quixotic, ego-driven bid for the presidency. A lot of people laughed at him, rolling their eyes when he said his supporters would let him get away with shooting someone on Fifth Avenue.

It was a sign that Americans were living in two different realities.

The truth is, they had been for a long time. But those realities had become so estranged from one another, each existing in its own separate bubble, that those who lived in Obamaworld were barely aware that another world still existed. If they did, they dismissed it as fading and irrelevant, ignoring what Trump recognized as a sleeping giant.

In reality, the signs were all there. In 2013, at the outset of Obama's second term, conservative political hosts occupied seven of the top eight positions in Talkers magazine's "Heavy Hundred." Limbaugh and Hannity led the way, with stalwarts like Glenn Beck, Michael Savage, and Mark Levin also making the list.

In 2015, Fox News was the most popular channel on cable: not just the most popular news channel, but the most popular channel *period*, easily outdrawing the likes of ESPN, the Hallmark Channel, and Turner Broadcasting.

Emboldened in their own bubble, they were speaking out more forcefully and stridently against the perceived evils of political correctness, secularism, and liberalism. The election of Obama, seen as a triumph of diversity and inclusion by some, was viewed by others as a source of discomfort or even an existential threat.

Looking back, Obama himself recognized it in his 2020 memoir.

"It was as if my very presence in the White House had triggered a deep-seated panic, a sense that the natural order had been disrupted," he wrote.

Vouching for Racism

Instead of representing the defeat of racism, Obama's election brought suppressed racist instincts back to the fore.

In truth, they'd been intertwined with various conservative priorities for some time. In the mid-20th century, far-right theologian R.J. Rushdoony had suggested that interracial marriage should be outlawed as "unequal yoking," that slavery had been "benevolent," and that some people were, in fact, slaves by nature.

The Civil War, he said, had destroyed the nation — not by dividing it, but because the South had lost. He saw the end of the Confederacy as a defeat for Christian orthodoxy.

Not surprisingly, Rushdoony sought to combat the secular public education system by providing an alternative via homeschooling. Public school was demonized as an instrument for liberal indoctrination (e.g., teaching children to think for themselves, rather than submitting to Christian doctrine).

Before long, this push expanded into a campaign for vouchers that could provide white Christians with "school choice" a new approach to preserving segregation.

The irony of this should not be lost: Evangelicals were arguing for the right to choose, even though many of them wanted to *deny* others this same right — by transforming the United States into a Christian state.

As they solidified their alliance with evangelicals, Republicans took up the cause, too, and for good reason: Private schools served as another "bubble" where they could insulate "their kind" from outsiders they saw as a threat. As a bonus, they provided a place to indoctrinate the next generation.

In the words of Proverbs: "Train of a child in the way he should go" so that "even when he is old, he will not depart from it."

(Opponents raised concerns that vouchers violated the separation of church and state. However, the Supreme Court ruled in 2002 that they were fine as long as families could choose either religious or nonreligious private schools.)

A bubble, whether it's a conservative Facebook group or a private religious school, serves two functions. One is to keep the faithful inside — to prevent them from straying. And the other is to keep the sinful world out — to avert any contamination by "the other."

It doesn't take much thought to realize how this kind of mindset can dovetail with racism. And, indeed, school choice has historically been used as an excuse to preserve racial segregation. After the Supreme Court ruled against the "separate but equal" principle in *Brown v. Board of Education*, conservatives responded by opening their own schools, which became known as segregation academies.

Jerry Falwell, later the founder of the Moral Majority (and a champion of school choice), was at the forefront of this effort. He railed against *Brown v. Board* in a one of his sermons, declaring that "the facilities should be separate."

"The true Negro does not want integration," Falwell asserted. "He realizes his potential far better among his own race."

Falwell put his money where his mouth was, establishing Liberty Christian Academy in Lynchburg, Virginia, as a "private school for white students" in 1967.

Seventeen years later, he expressed even greater disdain for another minority group, condemning the gay-friendly Metropolitan Community Church for operating what he called "a vile and satanic system" that would one day be "utterly annihilated."

Lines of Distinction

Falwell was not alone. By 1969, there were more than 200 private segregation academies operating across the South. Seven states offered vouchers to help families pay tuition — effectively incentivizing them to keep schools segregated. In Mississippi alone, 41,000 students moved from public schools to segregation academies in 1970-71.

Court-ordered efforts to integrate schools by busing students from inner-city schools to suburban campuses, and vice versa, outraged white parents in places like Boston and Los Angeles. Some were upset that their kids had to spend hours on a bus each day; others feared the quality of education at inner-city schools was inferior; still others didn't want their children attending classes with "those people."

These diverse motivations galvanized many in white America at large to support the kind of private-school alternative backed by evangelicals.

Ironically, while conservatives pushed for government money to keep schools segregated in the South, they sought to maintain a different form of segregation in the West by *withholding* public dollars. In 1994, California voters passed Proposition 187, which would have denied public funds for education, health care, and other services to undocumented immigrants. (The law was challenged in court and never took effect.)

It was all about maintaining a barrier between the "in" group and outsiders. Building a wall, so to speak. In religious terms, those on the outside were heretics and unbelievers. In social terms, they were those with different racial, ethnic, and cultural backgrounds. But for many conservative evangelicals, they were one and the same.

Not only did walls keep "undesirables" out, it enabled believers to tell the difference between the chosen and the damned. This was a crucial aspect of their raison d'être, and Falwell didn't even bother trying to hide it. On the contrary, he invoked the name of God in an effort to justify it.

"When God has drawn a line of distinction, we should not attempt to cross that line," he said, warning that integration would "destroy our race eventually." He seemed appalled at the fact that, in one northern city, a "couple of opposite race" lived next door to a fellow pastor's church.

As though this were the end of the world.

Lines of distinction had to be drawn. If they weren't at some point, there would be no way to tell the sheep from the goats — whether you were talking in spiritual or racial terms. And then you'd have to come to terms with the fact that the two really weren't all that different.

That was something people like Falwell could never accept. It would deprive them of their feeling that they were special. Chosen. Superior. It's the same kind of conceit that fueled the horrors of apartheid, Naziism, and, on American soil, justified slavery, conquest, and nationalist arrogance. It's the idea that "we know better because we *are* better."

Above the Law

This feeling of "special status" was nothing new. It had surfaced in the mid-1800s under the name Manifest Destiny, a doctrine that sought to justify the conquest of North America as the will of God.

That, of course, meant displacing native tribes, either by force or treaty — and tearing up those treaties after they'd signed them, because (don't you know) the rules applied to others, not to them.

This is an attitude typical of "chosen" people: Whether they're members of royal, wealthy, or religious elite classes, they believe they're above the law. They love to portray themselves as advocates for morality or law and order, but only when such concepts apply to those below them in the pecking order.

As part of the privileged class, they make the rules, but they don't have to keep them, because the rules have only one real purpose: to keep everyone beneath them in their place. If they can get less-privileged classes to buy into those rules, based on the false promise that they'll be rewarded by doing so, they can solidify their own standing (and benefit from cheap labor to boot).

Little had changed in the 21st century, when Donald Trump eagerly withdrew from agreements signed by his predecessors, such as the Iran nuclear treaty and Paris Climate Accord, with the same fervor that 19th century Americans had torn up tribal treaties.

It's also not surprising that his critics accused him of putting himself above the law.

Another outgrowth of the "chosen" mentality is a concept called American exceptionalism — which is really little more than nationalism in a specifically American context. It's the mentality that led Ronald Reagan to declare the United States was a "shining city on a hill" in his 1989 farewell address.

Like Manifest Destiny, this reference had religious backing. It was based on Jesus' words in the Gospel of Matthew: "You are the light of the world. A city on a hill cannot be hidden." So, not only was America a beacon set *above* the rest of the world, it had God's implicit sanction to serve as such.

In choosing this specific wording, Reagan was affirming his evangelical allies' narrative by suggesting the United States was a Christian nation. But not just that: *the* Christian nation. He was suggesting that America was the ultimate expression of Christianity: the kingdom of God on earth.

Everyone else was beneath us, looking up.

And because we've already reached the pinnacle, the implication is, we have nothing to learn from anyone "out there" or "down below," because they're either less enlightened Christians who can't teach us anything us or godless heathens who have nothing worthwhile to say. Such barbarians are all inferior, because everything worth knowing is contained in the Bible, pastors' sermons and church dogma.

This attitude goes to the heart of evangelical dogma. Critics might call it a spirit of pride or arrogance, and you know what the Book of Proverbs says about that: "Pride goeth before destruction, and a haughty spirit before a fall." If you're a city on a hill, there's nowhere to go but down.

But those who emphasize position over all else have little use for such ethical teachings. As mentioned, they don't think they're bound by them: They're meant to keep the lower classes in their place.

This helps explain why there are two sorts of Christianity. One is humble, focusing inward; the other is boldly evangelical, looking outward.

Both traditions are found in Christian scripture, although the former is more closely linked to the New Testament. "Gentle Jesus, meek and mild" counseled his followers not to pray in public to gain the approval of men, but to do so in secret, behind closed doors. This would seem to suggest a private, inward faith. Yet Jesus the evangelist told his followers to "go into all the world and preach the good news."

He also told his followers that he would deny them before his heavenly father if they dared to deny *him* before men.

But did words really matter that much?

In fact, Jesus warned of wolves in sheep's clothing and told his followers they would be known by their fruits — not, he implied, by empty words. His kingdom, he explicitly said, was "not of this world." This would seem to suggest a faith built on an inner communion with God that manifests itself as a positive example, which others will be drawn to follow.

But there's another way of looking at the difference between these two strands of Christianity. One emphasizes the teachings of Jesus, who told his followers that "if anyone loves me, he will keep my word, and the Father will love him." The other focuses on loyalty to the *person* of Jesus, rather than the ideals he espoused: "Whoever is not with me is against me."

Republicans and their evangelical allies have long decried "identity politics." But personal loyalty, when valued over and above fidelity to a cause or principle, is the epitome of that concept.

Cult of Personality

Flash forward to the 21st century.

We'll explore how evangelical views of the gospel paved the way for Donald Trump in more depth later, but their emphasis on faith — and his on loyalty — at the expense of moral teachings and principles bears exploring briefly here.

From the beginning, Trump has cast himself as a person whose relationships are defined by loyalty, not principle. They're entirely transactional and wholly personal. If you praise him, he praises you. If you're critical, he eviscerates you via Twitter or on Fox.

A few examples:

Anthony Scaramucci, who served briefly as Trump's press secretary, went from being "an important addition to this administration" to a "highly unstable 'nut job'" after he turned on Trump.

Chief of Staff John Kelly started out as "a very talented man," only to be slammed on his departure as someone who was in "way over his head."

Jim Mattis went from being "a man of honor, a man of devotion, and a man of total action" to "the world's most overrated general."

And Jeff Sessions, once lauded as "a man of integrity, a man of principle" wound up being castigated as an unqualified "disaster as attorney general."

What does the "gospel of Trump" have in common with the teachings of Jesus?

Not much.

In dealing with an aggressor, Jesus counseled his followers to "turn the other cheek," while Trump said he'd "like to punch him in the face."

Regarding empathy, Jesus said, "Blessed are those who mourn." Faced with thousands of people dying from coronavirus, Trump stated: "People are dying. It is what it is."

Jesus: "You cannot serve two masters, God and money." Trump: "If you don't support me, you'll be so goddamn poor."

Jesus: "I was a stranger, and you invited me in." Trump: "Build the wall!"

Trump was talking about a wall along the Mexican border. But more broadly, he sought a wall of separation between the cities and the suburbs, people of color and white Americans, the wealthy and the poor. His divisive politics no doubt felt familiar to evangelicals operating from a similar template — one that divided the saved and the damned, the beloved and the cursed, the righteous from the sinners, the elect from the condemned.

Love thy neighbor?

Not a chance. They preferred to focus on the divisive side of Jesus' teachings: "Do not think that I came to bring peace on earth; I came not to bring peace, but a sword. For I came to set a man against his father, and a daughter against her mother, and a daughter-in-law against her mother-in-law. And a man's enemies will be the members of his own household."

He might as well have been describing the age of Trump. Across America, families in 2020 were divided by conflict between supporters and foes of the 45th president. Friendships were similarly strained — or ruined. Barely 1 in 10 registered voters said they had more than a few close friends who supported the other party's candidate for president. Nearly 60% of Trump boosters and almost half of Joe Biden's supporters said they had *zero* close friends in the opposite camp.

Welcome to the bubble.

"We don't like to kill our unborn; we need them to grow up and fight in our wars."

Marilyn Manson,
singer and songwriter

Abortion Distortions

Before going any further, it's important to consider the role abortion has played in the evangelical movement. It's a difficult topic to discuss, because opinions are so intense on both sides of the issue. But that's part of what makes it essential to examine the role it has played in shaping evangelical leaders' approach to politics and power.

Abortion is, more than anything else, the issue that defines and galvanizes the evangelical movement.

It seems like it's been that way forever.

Politically, opposition to abortion has become all but synonymous with evangelical Christianity. In 2018, there were ten Christian denominations where more than 50% of congregants thought abortion should be illegal. Seven of them were evangelical.

Prominent among them: The Cleveland, Tenn.-based Church of God at 77%, the Assemblies of God at 71%, and the Southern Baptist Convention — the nation's largest evangelical denomination — at 66%.

Overall, nearly twice as many evangelicals opposed legal abortion than supported it. And opposition isn't just widespread among evangelicals, it's also fervent. Indeed, it would be natural to assume 1) that it had always been this way and 2) that it was fundamental to scripture or accepted dogma.

But neither of those assumptions is true. There's nothing in the Bible about abortion, per se. The closest thing to it is an Old Testament ban on a man "spilling his seed" — a clear reference to masturbation, not abortion.

Even more surprising: Evangelical opposition to abortion is a relatively recent phenomenon. In fact, the initial reaction to *Roe v. Wade* among evangelicals was actually *positive*. By the time the Supreme Court rendered its landmark ruling, the Southern Baptist Convention had already passed a resolution in 1971 supporting the right to an abortion.

It reaffirmed that stance not once but twice after the 1973 decision: the following year and again in 1976. At the time, evangelicals saw abortion as primarily a Catholic issue — and many of them were distrustful of or even hostile to the Catholic Church. Besides, support for abortion rights was consistent with conservative views on small government and states' rights.

Many conservatives had backed these views as a way to preserve segregation against what they saw as federal interference. This was especially true in the South, but it wasn't as big an issue elsewhere, at least outside of big cities that were dealing with court-ordered busing. To the rest of the country, "segregation academies" like the one operated by Jerry Falwell in Virginia, seemed backward and racist. Southern evangelical leaders wanted a way to get tax-exempt status for their all-white schools — something the courts had denied them, ruling that they were discriminatory. An even better option: school vouchers, which would funnel money directly into religious (mostly white) schools.

In order to gain support, however, they needed a broader-based cause: something that would appeal to conservatives outside the South. That cause turned out to be opposition to abortion. As the number of abortions began to rise, conservative activist Paul Weyrich (who had founded the Heritage Foundation in 1973) began to notice unease among conservatives was rising, as well.

He realized this might just be the issue to unite the evangelical base.

When he joined forces with Falwell to form the Moral Majority in 1979, the pair made it a signature issue in their alliance with Ronald Reagan.

To most evangelicals, stopping abortions was a worthy goal in and of itself, but to leaders like Falwell and Weyrich, it was a means to an end: They wanted to transform the United States into a Christian nation, or, to put it another way, to make America great again.

As Weyrich wrote in the mid-1970s, "The new political philosophy must be defined by us in moral terms, packaged in non-religious language, and propagated throughout the country by our new coalition. When political power is achieved, the moral majority will have the opportunity to re-create this great nation."

Opposition to abortion became the cornerstone of a "family values" agenda pushed by evangelicals in opposition to feminism,

LGBTQ rights, and, of course, racial integration. Encouraging the faithful to "be fruitful and multiply" fulfilled a biblical directive, but it did a couple of other things, too.

First, it reinforced the idea of a nuclear family based on the union of one man and one woman, over and against alternative (read: same-sex) models.

Second, it encouraged white evangelicals to have children so they could perpetuate religious traditions — with the help of parochial schools, of course — that they believed to be in danger.

Evangelical leaders were dismayed by the influx of immigrants, particularly people of color who followed traditions such as Catholicism and Islam that they believed posed a threat to their way of life.

The fact that many of these immigrants were having more babies than white evangelicals compounded the problem. It was therefore in leaders' interests to encourage their followers to have larger families. Banning abortions was one way to achieve this goal.

It might seem cynical to suggest that evangelical leaders' pro-life position was a stepping stone to political power. Certainly, many rank-and-file evangelicals feel passionately and sincerely about this issue (as do others outside this tradition, by the way). But the indifference of evangelical leaders and their conservative allies toward children once they're out of the womb — and toward their mothers — tells a different story.

They've regularly argued against providing assistance for children in low-income families. And that's revealing.

It's far easier to pass "thou shalt not" laws, Old Testament style, than it is to provide the kind of grace and compassion Jesus talked about in the gospels. But it's not nearly as effective.

If evangelicals truly wanted to discourage abortion, one of the best ways of doing so would be to keep women from feeling like they were on their own in raising their children. If the state has a compelling interest in keeping children alive in the womb, it has an equally compelling interest in ensuring they're safe and secure when they're born into a much more threatening environment outside.

And that interest goes far beyond indoctrinating them in a specific religious tradition. The willingness of some conservatives to separate immigrant children from their parents and put them in cages along the southern border reveals their true priority: It's not life, and it's not children. It's preserving the racial/cultural status quo.

As writer Tom Zirpoli put it: "As long as someone else is carrying them, pro-lifers can be very generous when it comes to their concern for the unborn. It costs them nothing and they don't need to do anything except write 'pro-life' on their campaign materials. Once children are born, however, they need food and a place to sleep. Sometimes, they need medicine. All of this costs money. Protecting the life of the unborn is far cheaper and easier than caring for them after they are born."

Even more jarring, evangelical leaders who describe themselves as pro-life are often "hawks" who promote the idea of sending young people overseas to fight in the military. Many of them also favor the death penalty.

The hypocrisy is jarring.

But hypocrisy can cut both ways: Those who oppose the death penalty and sending young people to fight overseas often favor abortion rights and right-to-die laws. It can be argued that there's no consistency there, either.

The goal, however, shouldn't be to condemn the hypocrisy on either side. Rather, it should be to bring *both sides* together so they can discuss issues that are far more complex than either seems willing to admit.

Unfortunately, this has become all but impossible because each has backed itself into a dogmatic corner.

And that's unfortunate.

The "pro-life" stance has become all but synonymous with religious conservatism, while the "pro-choice" view became the dominant symbol of the women's rights movement, eclipsing issues such as equal pay, violence against women, and equal opportunity.

Indeed, the underlying issues surrounding abortion are complicated, and strong arguments exist on both sides of the issue. The *Roe* decision set a standard based on the three trimesters of pregnancy: During the first, governments could prohibit all abortions; during the second, they could set reasonable health rules; during the third, they could ban abortions altogether except to protect the life or health of the mother.

But another decision in 1992 upended this standard, replacing it with fetal viability: Could the child survive outside the uterus? And that question has been answered differently as science — and survivability — have improved.

Still, outside the courts, civil discussion of the issue became all but impossible. Compromise is a dirty word to many evangelicals, who have come to view the pro-life position as an article of faith and a core component of their identity — even though barely one-third (35%) of mainline Protestants currently share their position.

Women's rights groups, meanwhile, have come to view reproductive choice as the defining issue of *their* movement, a stance that can never be questioned. Instead of engaging in a dialogue based on science and ethics, the two sides have retreated into their respective corners, encased in dogma and worried that any discussion would send them down a slippery slope into the enemy camp — where they're sure they'd be ambushed by hostile forces.

Each side is stuck on opposite sides of an invisible wall; each trapped in its own bubble, listening only to preachers addressing their respective choirs, and shouting at "enemies" they're sure could never understand.

"A little hyperbole never hurts."

Donald J. Trump,
The Art of the Deal, 1987

Messianic Mindset

Donald Trump knew how to use the us-versus-them mindset to his advantage. He understood how the evangelical system worked, because he'd been an evangelist himself all his life: preaching the gospel of his own greatness to anyone who would listen.

Hyperbole was the name of the game. Marketing was his trademark — and promoting his brand was his greatest talent, whether there was any substance behind the hype or not. More often than not, there wasn't.

Trump's approach fit perfectly into the evangelical template. The only difference was that, instead of preaching the "good news" about Jesus, he was spreading his own messianic myth.

Trump didn't want anything to do with Jesus' paradoxical platitudes and beatitudes. "He who humbles himself will be exalted"? What a load of bull. Trump took the opposite approach: If he exalted himself enough, people would start to believe it.

And they did.

Jesus had warned his followers about people like Trump: "False messiahs and false prophets will arise and perform great signs and wonders, so as to lead astray, if possible, even the elect."

Apparently, it was — possible, that is.

The prophet Daniel had foreseen the rise of "a contemptible person to whom royal majesty has not been given" who "shall come without warning and obtain the kingdom by flatteries."

Whether one believes in prophecy or not, the point is that Christians *do* believe them, but seem not to have applied them to Trump: a man to whom royal majesty had not been given (he was a president, not a king) and who had hijacked the evangelical kingdom of God by flattering its leaders. And by insisting on being flattered himself.

Instead of appealing to God for authority, Trump appealed to his own supposed expertise, declaring "I alone can fix it," and boasting that he knows more about (fill in the blank) than anybody else.

The justice system.

Trade.

Taxes.

Renewable energy.

Technology.

Infrastructure.

Money.

The courts.

Terrorists.

And the list goes on. According to Trump, he was the ultimate expert on everything; his followers need look no further than his judgment, because he had all the answers. If it sounds like Trump was setting himself up as God, that's exactly what he was doing — without ever quite coming out and saying it. He wasn't denigrating God the Father or Jesus or the Holy Spirit, but he wasn't giving them any credit, either. He wasn't like the quarterback who scores a touchdown and points to the sky or the slugger who crosses himself after sending the ball into the stands.

Trump didn't say he was the second coming, because that wouldn't have been good enough for his ego. He had to be the only one, because the world wasn't big enough for Jesus and Trump. If the carpenter from Nazareth had been a contestant on Trump's reality show, *The Apprentice*, Trump would have no doubt relished the opportunity to tell him, "You're fired!"

The irony of that show is that Trump never thought he needed an apprentice — someone who might offer him real advice — because he already thought he knew it all.

Like God.

108

And his followers, by extension, were the elect: true believers called by their very nature to believe in the gospel of Trump. Their role was to shower him with praise, in much the same way evangelical churchgoers lift their hands and voices to the almighty on Sunday morning. He told them they had "good genes," invoking the traditional narrative about a chosen race originally applied to the Jewish people and, subsequently, to the Christian church.

Trump was hijacking the Christian template and setting himself in Jesus' place as messiah — not openly, perhaps, but he was coming just about as close as he could without putting his foot over the line.

And hoping no one would notice.

His followers, who numbered in the tens of millions, didn't seem to. They accepted his ego-driven rhetoric because it fit the template for their faith they were already using. It was simple enough to substitute Trump for Jesus. In fact, it made perfect sense, because Trump was offering them something Jesus never could: an earthly kingdom.

And something else, as well: victory over their enemies.

Seeking Scapegoats

Trump's unlikely triumph in the 2016 election furthered his reputation as a miracle-worker, as did his recovery after being infected with the coronavirus. Jesus might have walked on water, but he'd never done anything like that. In fact, unlike Trump, he'd failed to set up an earthly kingdom... and had been crucified for trying. Trump had survived a deadly virus, but had Jesus survived the cross? Sure, he'd risen from the dead, but Trump had done just about the same thing by beating COVID (even if the survival rate for the virus was 97%).

He wasn't Jesus, he was Superman.

The suggestion that Trump was somehow better than Jesus is, of course, blasphemous to any orthodox Christian. That's why no one would say it out loud. But the fact is, a lot of evangelicals are more attracted to power in the present than a humble servant from the past.

"There's kind of a paradox in evangelical life," said Mark Galli, former editor of *Christianity Today*, told CBS News. "On the one hand, they're very suspicious of human authority, because the Bible is the word of God, and that's the ultimate authority. (But) on the other hand, the more conservative evangelical you are, the more you tend to get attracted to authoritarian figures.

"That might be preachers, and often it's government leaders. So, Trump has that swagger — he has kind of a charisma for that group of people."

They might not say so, but many evangelicals would rather have a conquering hero to enable their worse impulses than a scapegoat who died for their sins.

Villains are supposed to die, not heroes. So, they'd rather make someone *else* the scapegoat:

someone outside their bubble; on the other side of the wall they've built to protect their own sense of spiritual, cultural, and racial purity (read: superiority).

They know instinctively that villains are necessary to any good story, and they've created them throughout history among those who didn't look like them and/or share their beliefs. Native peoples hadn't heard of Jesus because God hadn't chosen *them* to receive his gospel; they were therefore savages, barbarians, and heathens.

Inherently inferior.

Some considered them less than human. They were enemies to be conquered and subdued, because they lived outside the wall that separated the saved from the condemned. Their only hope was to submit to the church and, in doing so, save their souls. This didn't, however, mean they would merit equality — or even save their lives. Those who recanted (at times under torture) might be killed anyway, for fear that they were doing so only to save their skins. Those accused of

witchcraft might have to be drowned to prove
they weren't witches.

Talk about a Catch-22.

The point is, there was something inherently
wrong with them that couldn't be tolerated,
because they came from the outside. They might
be exploited as cheap labor — whether they were
abducted from Africa or brought across the border
by human smugglers — but they would never be
accepted. In fact, their purpose was not just to
shoulder the burdens of hard labor, but the blame
for anything that went wrong.

As long as believers had someone to blame
who stood below them on the ladder, they
wouldn't look up at those in power who were
profiting off of *them*: priests and kings in the
Middle Ages; politicians, corporations, and
evangelists in the modern era.

Salvation doesn't mean much unless there's
something to be saved from. And regardless of
what Christian doctrine might say, it's a lot easier
to blame than ask forgiveness. It's much less painful

to point out someone else's supposed flaws than to focus on your own shortcomings and sins.

White evangelicals not only needed a messiah, they needed a devil — and not just an abstract, amorphous spiritual devil. They needed flesh-and-blood enemies: people who weren't like them. They had their own scapegoats before Trump came along. Trump didn't supply any new ones. What he did was simply support them in their animus toward those who they perceived as threats.

He not only enabled their most aggressive impulses, he goaded them on with crude name-calling and vindictive behavior. They didn't like immigrants, so he vowed to "build the wall." They couldn't stand Democratic nominee Hillary Clinton, who they saw as an insult added to the injury of her African-American predecessor. So he chanted, "Lock her up!"

He used simple chants and slogans that played on fears and pent-up frustrations. It's no wonder that those frustrations burst into the open.

Evangelicals and their allies now had permission to express them. They no longer had to keep them bottled up for fear of being condemned as uncivil or politically incorrect.

Trump, they said, told the truth.

Actually, he *lied* about the facts more than anybody else, but that wasn't what mattered. What mattered was the truth of the emotions they felt, the feelings that they were being victimized and disrespected by a corrupt and evil world. And he told them what they wanted to hear.

He also rode the winds of change.

Once upon a time, the Republican Party had cast Russia as its villain of choice in a struggle of good vs. evil. Fear of the USSR had served as the basis of Joseph McCarthy's "red scare" campaign to purge the nation of alleged Soviet agents and sympathizers. The policy of containment had targeted Russian ambition and led to American involvement in the deadly morass that was the Vietnam War.

But the end of the Cold War had left the
United States as the world's lone superpower —
and without a devil: a convenient villain to blame
and censure. By the time Trump arrived on the
scene, the Cold War was long past, and Russia was
no longer "communist" — a word that still carried
pejorative power, even though the Soviet Union
was long gone.

Trump had no interest in keeping Russia as a
scapegoat. His reasons were unclear. It might have
been his apparent hero worship of strongman
Vladimir Putin, his desire to promote his own
business interests in Russia, his reluctance to admit
that Russia had helped him win the presidency,
some combination of these factors, or something
else entirely. Regardless, he was motivated to
remove Russia from the list of Republican
scapegoats, and he sensed that the time was right
to do so.

He met every suggestion that Russia was
involved in meddling with U.S. elections by
deflecting the blame to China, which he viewed as

an economic threat. But because China wasn't a *physical* threat to the United States, he had to come up with other scapegoats, as well. He found two of them. The first were Muslims, who he blamed en masse for the 9/11 terrorist attacks and sought to bar from entering the nation. The second were Hispanic immigrants, who he warned were heading north in massive caravans of drug dealers, criminals, and rapists intent on invading the country.

He'd build a wall to keep them out, and (in an absurd piece of fiction), he insisted Mexico would pay for it.

He told the people what they want to hear.

He'd "drain the swamp" of corrupt Washington insiders like Hillary Clinton, and never mind his own legacy of corruption (Trump University, anyone?). If he broke the rules, that was just a way of fighting fire with fire. If he gamed the system and paid less than his fair share of taxes, that just proved he was smart.

Yes, he was a bully, but that's exactly what they wanted: someone to fight dirty for them in a conflict they felt like they were losing. They'd been waiting for God to send them a savior, and Trump appeared to be the answer to their prayers.

He promised them the one thing they craved more than anything.

Not a principled Christian life.

Not even God's approval.

He promised them they were going to win.

Hollow Victories

"We're gonna win so much," he vowed, "you may even get tired of winning. And you'll say, 'Please, please, it's too much winning. We can't take it anymore. Mr. President, it's too much.' And I'll say, 'No it isn't. We have to keep winning. We have to win more! We're gonna win more!'"

Of course, no one wins all the time. Politicians make promises they fail to keep, and Trump is no different. But his *response* was different, and it was exactly the type of response evangelicals had come to expect.

From God and his ministers.

Trump doesn't admit he's fallen short. He pretends he's succeeded. He shouts it from the rooftops. Then he keeps repeating it until people believe it, despite the evidence. Just like they believe the pastors who tell them that God has kept his promises, even though they're still in poverty or a being treated unfairly or dealing with the death of a loved one from some horrible disease.

Don't look at the evidence. Have faith. Believe God.

Trump used the very same formula, but he substituted his own name for that of the Almighty, and in so doing, he imposed an alternate reality on his followers. He told them what they wanted to believe, whether it was true or not. Some people might say he sold them a bill of goods.

The evidence be damned.

Literally.

Have you ever wondered why some evangelicals fight so hard to discredit (or simply ignore) scientific evidence? It would seem simple enough to believe, for example, that God used evolution as a tool to fashion the world as we know it; that the six-day creation story was an allegory. Or a parable, Jesus' favored form of teaching.

Their stubborn refusal to do so seems inexplicable — until you realize that evangelicals operate largely in a black-and-white universe, where compromise is a dirty word and conflict between the forces of light and the armies of darkness is fundamental to their way of viewing the world... just as conflict is fundamental to Trump's way of doing things.

Again, it all fits. For Trump, it's conflict that gives live meaning, and victory that affirms his own sense of self-worth. Similarly, evangelicals affirm their own status as the chosen ones by contrasting themselves with the forces of evil — and vanquishing them.

Not by compromising with them.

To evangelicals, the truth is absolute and the Bible is inerrant — two cornerstones of evangelical belief. There can be no truth to the "other side," even if there's scientific evidence to back it up. Perhaps especially then, because evidence removes the need for faith.

And as the author of Hebrews says, "without faith, it is impossible to please God."

Of course, faith means different things do different people. One could easily argue that it takes just as much faith to believe God created an evolving universe as it would to believe in a literal six-day process. But evangelical faith is a different *kind* of faith.

It isn't faith that God can work through the laws of creation, but in spite of them. It doesn't make much sense, if you think about it, to believe that God would create a world governed by natural laws just so he could violate them on a whim, but that's at the heart of evangelical belief.

Natural processes are mundane. Miracles are the big show, the evidence that god exists.

And since miraculous evidence violates natural laws, it's at odds with the evidence provided by science.

Checkmate.

To the evangelical, explaining the way things are rationally robs God of his mystery and, indeed, his autonomy. The price of such a belief — one that depends on God's capriciousness to provide proof of his existence — is high. It requires a sense of chaos and instability that can only be offset by the fiercest loyalty... which is, in fact, what this sort of faith is.

It is, in fact, the very sort of no-questions-asked, yes-man faith demanded by Donald Trump. In exchange, he provides (you guessed it) chaos. While those on the outside find that chaos exhausting, his loyal followers find it comforting. It's evidence he's in control, that he can do miracles, that he's not constrained by the sort of natural laws that apply to everyone else.

Is it any wonder that Trump denounces science on climate change, for example? It's not that he doesn't believe it, per say, he just thinks he's above it. The same goes for the coronavirus, which he managed to survive — and subsequently downplayed.

"If I can get better," he boasted, "anyone can get better."

All you have to do is have faith.

You can almost hear the faint echo of Jesus' words in Trump's declaration: "Truly, truly, I say to you: Whoever believes in me will also do the works that I do; and greater works than these will he do, because I'm going to the father."

It's doubtful that Trump himself ever read this quotation, and his meaning was no doubt quite different than what Jesus intended. Lost in Trump's translation is the humility of Jesus' statement, downplaying his own works and trusting in the Father as the source of all things.

Trump would probably take a different lesson from the scripture. He'd likely view it, as he does most things, in transactional terms: If you achieve something (even with the help of the best doctors and experimental treatments), offer it to your followers as a gift to increase their faith. Their loyalty.

Would his followers see the distinction? Some might; others probably wouldn't. But either way, they'd hear something that sounds vaguely familiar, that would put them at ease because it sounded like something Jesus *might* say.

But there's a huge difference between Trump and the Jesus of the gospels. Jesus called out the Pharisees for doing just the sort of things Trump seems to revel in: for taking the best seats at public meetings; for boasting loudly about their virtues; for promoting an image at odds with their real nature.

"You cleanse the outside of the cup and dish, but inside you are filled with greed and wickedness," he told them.

Jesus downplayed miracles, too. He told a parable of seed scattered on shallow soil, which sprang up quickly but soon withered in the hot sun because it had no roots. A faith based on miracles was like that: shallow and misplaced. "A wicked and adulterous situation looks for a sign," he told the Pharisees. "Yet no sign will be given but the sign of Jonah."

What was the sign of Jonah? Contrary to popular belief, it wasn't a miracle. Jonah had gone to the Ninevites to warn them they were on the road to destruction. They hadn't needed a miracle, but had listened to his warning and heeded his words, based simply on their merit.

One wonders what Jesus might say to Trump's followers, and whether they would listen.

It appears doubtful.

After all, the Pharisees didn't.

STEPHEN H. PROVOST

"If you don't choose heroes, heroes will be chosen for you, and they will not represent values that empower you, they will represent powers that will enslave you."

Russell Brand,
English actor/comedian

Donald and Bathsheba

Why have so many evangelicals stood by Donald Trump in the face of actions that seem to be directly at odds with the teachings of the Bible?

When it comes right down to it, as much as they talk about sin, *specific* sins are of much less concern to many evangelicals than the "work of the devil." Sins themselves are viewed as inevitable, because each of us is — according to a doctrine set forth by the Apostle Paul — born into a fallen state because of Adam's original sin.

"We're all sinners," Jerry Falwell Jr., son of the Moral Majority founder, said in announcing he was still supporting Trump, despite allegations of immorality and racism. Falwell, in fact, declared that Trump "does not have a racist bone in his body" — an assertion that seems preposterous coming from the son of a religious segregationist.

But sinful acts, whether they're racism, fornication, or whatever, can be forgiven, and Christians will still sin. So the endgame isn't to stop people from sinning, it's to redeem their fallen nature and make sure the devil doesn't tempt them back to what Darth Vader might call "the dark side."

Take the story of the woman at the well in the Gospel of John, who had already been married five times and was living with a man outside of wedlock. Jesus made note of this, but he didn't condemn her for it. Instead, he used it as an opportunity to identify himself as the messiah — the rightful ruler of Israel and the kingdom of God.

This was the point of the passage, and it's the point evangelicals are focused on, too. They're far less concerned about sinful acts (individual transgressions against God or his people) than they are about humanity's sinful nature as defined by the Apostle Paul and the salvation from it they believe Jesus can provide.

Remember, evangelicals believe they're engaged in a black-and-white struggle between the forces of good and evil. Salvation and damnation. God and Satan. The sin of Adam and the redemption of the "second Adam," Jesus.

American politics represents a convenient parallel to the good-vs.-evil struggle of the evangelical mindset because, like the dualist battle between God and Satan, the U.S. electoral system typically presents voters with two choices. It's easy for evangelicals to align those choices with the God's heavenly hosts and Satan's demonic hordes — the armies of light and darkness engaged in "spiritual warfare" on the eternal plane.

When the Republican Party co-opted the evangelical movement (or was it the other way around?) during the era of Jerry Falwell Sr.'s Moral Majority in the 1980s, the two became joined at the hip. Many evangelicals started to see Republicans as an earthly "army of light" corresponding to the heavenly host, while demonizing Democrats as tools of "the enemy."

This is likely why, in the minds of many evangelicals, Donald Trump can be forgiven for his undeniably sinful attitudes and actions toward women, while Bill Clinton cannot. No matter how many times Trump has engaged in fornication or boasted about abusive behavior, and no matter how many times he's switched parties or positions, he has been redeemed in the eyes of many evangelicals by his association with the Republican Party and the evangelical church. Clinton, on the other hand, is "outside the fold." Calling himself a Christian and asking forgiveness aren't good enough for evangelicals who have accepted the premise that the GOP is God's chosen instrument in U.S. politics. He might as well be an Irish Protestant asking forgiveness of the IRA.

Hero Worship

It's possible that evangelists recognized Trump as one of their own — and vice versa — *because* of how he acted, not in spite of it. Trump may not have been a "moral" person, but he spoke their language: the language of flattery, validation... and money.

Some found him even more welcoming that Ronald Reagan, who had forged the GOP alliance with evangelicals in the first place.

Reagan was "the first president who allowed evangelicals to have a seat at the table — he didn't listen to them that much, but he at least allowed them a seat at the table," said Dallas megachurch pastor Robert Jeffress, a Trump supporter. Trump, however, was "the first president who actually listened and incorporated some of the views of evangelicals in his policies."

But it's also possible that at least some evangelical leaders saw in Trump one of their own: a prosperity preacher and huckster who used faith (or loyalty) as a lever to create a cash cow in the tradition of faith healers and televangelists.

He promised things he couldn't deliver, then moved on to promise other things instead. He even took a page directly out of their playbook by touting "cures" for the coronavirus such as injecting bleach (bad idea), and unproven treatments like hydroxychloroquine and remdesivir. Or simply vowing that the virus would just go away "like a miracle."

Of course it didn't.

But that didn't stop him from declaring that one day, he would be right. It had to happen at some point, didn't it? (It was just a matter of how many people were infected and died in the meantime.)

It's no wonder that disgraced televangelists like Jim Bakker gravitated toward Trump, touting his own unproven COVID cures on his website, which got him in hot water with the state of Missouri. He also hawked a $45 prayer coin depicting Trump and the ancient Persian King Cyrus the Great, celebrated in the Bible for delivering Israel from the yoke of the Babylonian Empire. Cyrus is even explicitly called a "messiah" (anointed one) in the scripture.

And Bakker isn't the only evangelical leader who has fawned over Trump as though he were the second coming. Among those who hitched their fates to the reality TV star were Jeffress; Jerry Falwell Jr.; Georgia-based televangelist Jentezen Franklin; and early Moral Majority backer James Robison.

Franklin Graham claimed his father, famed evangelist Billy Graham, had "believed in" Trump and voted for him: "He believed Donald J. Trump was the man for this hour in history for our nation."

Mike Pence, who casts himself as a devout evangelical Christian, has been unwavering in his support for Trump. It's been speculated that Pence sees Trump as a means to a political end, and evangelical leaders have admitted they view him in the same light.

In supporting Trump, evangelical leaders made a deal with the devil that required them to treat him like a messiah. His moral conduct wasn't a factor in their decision one way or the other. Their support was purely transactional: You scratch my back, I'll scratch yours. It's Trump's language of choice, and it's easy for evangelists who've made plenty of money off their faith to understand.

To them, Trump wasn't sinning. In fact, it was just the opposite: He was being honest about who he was. "He never pretended to be a super Christian," Jentezen Franklin said. "He never pretended to be some holy saint."

Jeffress echoed those sentiments. "We weren't voting for him for his personal piety, but for his strong leadership," he said.

He recalled the day Trump invited him to Trump Tower: "We were friends instantly," he said. "Donald Trump has never been one to falsely portray himself as a pious individual, but he is an extremely strong leader."

Macho Men

That sense of machismo — even from someone who avoided serving in Vietnam and labeled war hero John McCain a "loser" — appealed to a lot of evangelicals. This was especially true for male leaders who saw feminism as a threat to the natural biblical order. As Paul had written, wives should be subject to their husbands, and it was shameful for a woman to speak in church.

Since most evangelicals believe in taking the Bible literally, it's no surprise that they go "by the book" when it comes to Paul's injunctions.

Indeed, the model of male leadership runs deep in evangelical churches, even if some now permit women to speak in their meetings. When they do, they typically affirm that their husbands and (male) pastors are the rightful leaders; their words are meant to lift these leaders up, not to express their own insights or opinions.

Evangelical men see women as subordinate, not just culturally, but because it's God's will. Husbands are, in Paul's words, expected to love their wives, just as Christ loved the church. But make no mistake: They hold the power, just as Jesus does, not by virtue of their moral virtue, but simply based on their identity. Their genitals.

This might help explain why so many evangelicals are willing to overlook Trump's abusive speech and behavior toward women: It's not his behavior that matters, but his role as a man and as head of the nation.

Trump's sexual boasting and inappropriate comments have been well documented. He's been known to leer at women and even underage girls, at one point suggesting that he might date his daughter if she weren't, well, his *daughter.*

Trump, who once owned Miss Universe, joked with radio shock jock Howard Stern that, as owner of the pageant, he might be under "obligation" to sleep with the contestants. But his behavior apparently went beyond what he would later describe as "locker room talk": He reportedly had a habit of entering changing rooms while contestants — some of whom were as young as 15 — were dressing. Some were topless or fully naked.

He sized them up as though he were judging entries at the state fair. One contestant, Miss Venezuela Alicia Machado, even said he called her "Miss Piggy" because she'd gained weight.

Over the years, he's called other women

dogs, fat pigs, and "horseface," invoking implicit ownership of them as though they were animals — even as he's maintained, "I love women." As long as they're attractive in his eyes, that is. As long as they fawn over him and don't make waves.

This would seem to be a glaring contradiction, but not to some evangelicals, who believe women are naturally subordinate to men and, as a result, should be subservient.

Trump reflected this mindset in a 2020 campaign rally, where he told women in the crowd that he was "getting your husbands back to work," reaffirming the Christian family-values model that placed the husband at the head of the household. He wasn't addressing women as individuals, but as junior partners whose success was tied to that of their husbands.

He appeared genuinely baffled that his message didn't seem to resonate with women in the suburbs, all but begging them: "Suburban women, will you please like me?" Apparently, he was oblivious to the fact that the suburbs had changed: They'd become more diverse, no longer the exclusive domain of white Christians. But that didn't mean his message stopped resonating with many white Christians. In fact, they ate it up.

Patriarchal Patterns

The patriarchal model had been part of the Christian faith tradition for millennia. The Catholic Church, for example, still stubbornly refuses to allow the ordination of women. But they bias dates back even further, to before Paul's writings: It's based on an Old Testament model that extended beyond families and small gatherings to the nation of Israel as a whole.

Israel wasn't a democracy. It was ruled by a king who was seen as God's chosen agent on Earth. The monarchy was a reflection of God's sovereignty in heaven, and as such was seen as the divinely ordained way of doing things.

In fact, Israel wasn't the only nation ruled by a king. In fact, monarchies were the rule across the ancient Near East. Nations had evolved (in fact, were still evolving) from older tribal states ruled by warrior-chieftains, who ascended by spilling blood more often by bloodlines.

Today, monarchies are the exception rather than the rule. Most modern states are governed by some form of democratic process, either as parliamentary or presidential republics. Some countries, like the U.K., retain monarchs as figureheads, but according to the CIA, only seven absolute monarchies remain — four of them on the Arabian Peninsula. (This doesn't include an assortment of strongmen, such as North Korea's Kim Jong Un, who resemble ancient kings more than modern monarchs.)

The reason: Kings tend to govern in their own interests, rather than their subjects'. Most nations have rejected that approach as inherently unfair and prone to cruelty. Power can corrupt, and power in the hands of those who are *already* corrupt is even worse.

The United States came to this conclusion at its founding. As Thomas Paine put it: "As in absolute governments, the king is law, so in free countries, the law ought to be king."

This aversion to tyranny in a nation that had rebelled against a king was understandable. But it's long been tempered by a sort of wistful yearning to have it both ways. Instead of royal families, we have political dynasties (the Adamses, the Harrisons, the Roosevelts, the Kennedys, the Bushes). And when government gets bogged down in gridlock, we elect "tough guy" leaders who can "get things done." Presidents like Teddy Roosevelt and Ronald Reagan, or governors like Jesse Ventura and Arnold Schwarzenegger.

Three of these leaders turned to politics after a career in acting (Schwarzenegger and Ventura actually appeared together in 1987's alien-invasion movie, *Predator*). All were throwbacks to the ancient tradition of a warrior chieftain.

The fact that their images were often media constructs — illusions — didn't keep the public from buying in. And Trump, a master of image and branding who'd forged a tough-guy image of his own on reality TV, was perfectly equipped to peddle the greatest illusion of all.

Especially to evangelicals.

He'd gotten out of serving in the military and, unlike Schwarzenegger and Ventura, wasn't a particularly impressive physical specimen. But Trump embraced the monarchical model that still held plenty of appeal for evangelicals — especially Dominionist thinkers and those frustrated at their declining clout within an increasingly diverse republic.

This was, to reiterate, the model represented in the Bible, with God ruling from a throne in heaven as and anointing kings to act in his behalf on earth (hence the title "king of kings" as opposed to "president of presidents").

The test of a king's legitimacy wasn't his righteousness, but his faithfulness to God. Fornication? No big deal. Solomon did it. David did it. But David continually recommitted himself to Yahweh, while Solomon earned the wrath of the prophets by allowing an Asherah pole — dedicated to a fertility goddess — to be placed in the temple of Yahweh.

In fact, if one wants to understand many evangelicals' continued embrace of Trump, one need look no further than David. Described in the Bible as a "man after God's own heart," he nonetheless slept with Bathsheba, the wife of a loyal soldier named Uriah. Then he sent Uriah to the front and arranged to have him slain in battle — clearing the way for David to marry Bathsheba.

Such actions were probably not unusual in the days when absolute monarchs could summon any woman to their bed. But they're less acceptable in the United States, which follows a model of government that owes its inspiration to

Greek democracy, not the ancient Near Eastern model of the tyrant king.

The tension between these two systems remains palpable for some evangelicals, who see their relationship to God as one of a subject to an absolute ruler and may view those they identify as God's chosen leaders in the same light.

So if Trump brags of being able to do anything he wants to a woman because he's "a star," he's boasting about something the Bible's most famous king, David, actually did.

Of course, not all evangelicals — and certainly not all Christians — think this way. There are plenty of people of faith who put morality ahead of what amounts to loyalty (remember Jesus' parable of one blind man leading another into a pit?). When then-Liberty University President Jerry Falwell Jr. announced he was still with Trump, a group of students at the university claiming to represent a majority of students and teachers on campus issued a statement denouncing Trump.

But that doesn't mean the behavior of evangelicals who have stuck by Trump is somehow inexplicable. In some ways, it makes perfect sense, and they really aren't as hypocritical as they might at first appear. They're just putting loyalty above morality and adhering to a model of government at odds with the representative democracy practiced in the U.S.

Is it surprising that they would gravitate toward a leader like Trump, who's more autocrat than democrat? Not at all. In fact, it's exactly what one would expect.

And it's no less surprising that they should support his efforts to overturn a free and fair election.

That's what a king would do.

"Ignorance and prejudice are the handmaidens of propaganda."

Kofi Annan,
U.N. Secretary-General, 1997-2006

Activating Prejudice

The civil rights era has come and gone, but racial segregation persists. Whether it's cultural or systemic (or both) is a question I'll leave for others. But plainly, it exists. If you have any doubt of this, look no further than the political affiliations in our nation's churches.

It may come as a surprise to some that church and faith play a larger role in the lives of Black Americans than they do for whites. According to Pew, 83% of African Americans are "absolutely certain" of their belief in God, compared with just

61% of whites. Blacks are more likely to pray, and nearly half attend church weekly, compared with roughly one-third of whites.

Yet by and large, they attend different churches. Evangelical Protestants churches are three-quarters white, while historically Black Protestant congregations are 94% African American.

And this has translated to the ballot box, where three-quarters of white evangelicals voted for Donald Trump in 2020, while four in five Black voters selected Joe Biden.

Most African-Americans aren't drawn in by Trump's pseudo-messianic posturing, perhaps because he panders to the same white evangelical crowd that sought to preserve segregation in the 1960s. Jerry Falwell Jr. was one of Trump's biggest supporters. And Trump even hired Mike Huckabee's daughter as his press secretary (although Huckabee himself has denounced racial segregation).

But Black voters were reliable supporters of Democrats long before Trump came along. In fact, they've been voting overwhelmingly for Democrats since way back in 1936, and Lyndon Johnson solidified that support even more with the Civil Rights Act of 1964.

But that same trend alienated white Southern Democrats, who began turning more toward the Republicans. Richard Nixon adopted a "Southern Strategy" explicitly to court them, and though the effect of this was blunted in 1968 by segregationist third-party candidate George Wallace, Nixon still won — and was re-elected by a landslide in 1972. Only Watergate and the Democratic candidacy of Southern Baptist favorite son Jimmy Carter in 1976 slowed the white Southern shift to the GOP (and even then, just temporarily).

Carter provided a bridge of sorts, in more ways than one — not just geographically and historically, but morally, as well. Carter, by all accounts, was an honorable and noble person. Unlike most politicians, he was honest to a fault, even admitting at one point that he'd "looked on a lot of women with lust."

At the time, it was seen as an unfortunate political gaffe: The consensus was that Carter had been *too* honest. Contrast that remark, however, with Donald Trump's crude boasts about being able to grab women "by the pussy." Some think Carter's words helped cut into his polling lead over Gerald Ford. And Jerry Falwell blasted him for sharing his story with Playboy, calling it a "salacious, vulgar magazine"... in an interview with Playboy's rival, Penthouse (although he claimed he didn't know it would appear there).

By contrast, Falwell's son — who later became embroiled in a sex scandal of his own — and other evangelicals stood by Trump after his coarse and abusive comments.

Things had changed.

And the transformation was set in motion by the elder Falwell, whose ironically named Moral Majority shifted evangelical priorities away from broad spiritual principles and toward the pursuit of earthly power. This power, he realized, could be attained if he activated evangelical outrage by pushing "hot buttons" — abortion, gay rights, feminism — that became go-to topics for the likes of Rush Limbaugh.

Falwell's efforts helped give birth to the "base" that would eventually elect Trump in 2016, having by this time become so obsessed with power that they'd abandoned any pretense of broad morality. Or, at least, viewed Trump's personal moral failings as less important than what he could deliver in terms of policy.

As Falwell Jr. put it, "You don't choose a president based on how good they are; you choose a president based on what their policies are. That's why I don't think it's hypocritical" to support Trump.

Evangelicals' deal with the devil was, as such deals generally are, purely transactional: just the kind that Trump thrived on. And it also fit in with the Republicans' business base. Transactions were, after all, at the core of capitalism.

To what extent was the white evangelical move to the GOP a reaction to the Black alliance with Democrats? Certainly, it was part of the initial motivation, a response to the civil rights and black power movements of the 1960s. But a half-century after Congress passed the Civil Rights Act, much of that impetus had been forgotten by broader society. They'd moved on from those white "grievances" even as they'd added insult to injury (from many white evangelicals' perspective) by building a broader coalition that included feminists, LGBTQ individuals, immigrants, minority faiths, and atheists.

Finding an Opening

As white evangelicals (and many white Americans in general) silently chafed at these developments, the assumption in "polite society" was that we'd moved past the ugly racism of the Jim Crow era — until that racism resurfaced in reaction to the most blatant challenge yet to white dominance: the election of a Black president. Champions of diversity viewed Barack Obama as the culmination of their drive for racial equality, but closeted racists saw it as just the opposite: potentially the final nail in their coffin.

In the 1960s, civil rights legislation had spurred a desperate bloc of racists voters to flee the Democratic Party in search of a solution to their worst nightmare. Now, almost 50 years later, Obama's election created a similar panic — and Donald Trump saw an opportunity.

If he could tap into this outrage, the way George Wallace and Richard Nixon had tapped into the segregationist backlash in 1968, he could activate latent white racism and ride its wave to power. Initially, he didn't think it would be enough to win the presidency, but like any savvy televangelist, he *did* think he could build a following — and make a profit off it.

He lucked out, however, when he drew Hillary Clinton as an opponent in 2016. She wasn't Black, but she represented another one of the right's nightmare scenarios: the triumph of feminism.

Clinton lacked some of the built-in advantages Obama had enjoyed. In 2008, the electorate had been ready for a change after eight years under Republican leadership — even more so because those eight years had concluded with the worse economic downturn since the Depression.

Obama was a relatively fresh face, having served just two years in the U.S. Senate when he launched his first campaign. He was best known for a rousing speech he'd delivered at the 2004 Democratic Convention, when he was just a state senator from Illinois.

Clinton, by contrast, had a long history as a controversial figure in Washington, having served as first lady, U.S. senator, and secretary of state. She'd been grilled repeatedly over her actions leading up to and in connection with a terrorist attack that killed four Americans in Libya.

She lacked Obama's charisma and had been repeatedly demonized by conservative pundits, making her unacceptable to a large number of voters — no matter who she ran against. Trump exploited her political baggage to the hilt, labeling her as "Crooked Hillary" Clinton and linking her to the corrupt Washington culture many conservatives hated.

Trump's name-calling wasn't new or original. He was actually taking a page out of Rush Limbaugh's playbook. Like Limbaugh, Trump was part political provocateur and part showman. And Like Limbaugh (who had condemned feminists as "feminazis") he dared to say things that many closet racists and sexists had been too scared to say themselves, for fear of the backlash.

The fact that he was vulgar and rude was actually a point in his favor, because it gave them permission to behave the same way — permission that had been denied them by a politically correct culture they viewed as unfair and oppressive. To them, Trump wasn't a mean-spirited bully, he was a champion of free speech and a fierce opponent of censorship. The very fact that he was willing to say extremely bad things only proved his dedication to the cause. And it increased their dedication to him.

When he pledged to make America great again, he was promising them a trip back to the Jim Crow era, reigniting Nixon's Southern strategy and applying it to rural areas nationwide. He even welcomed assistance from a self-proclaimed Nixonian "dirty trickster" named Roger Stone — and commuted his sentence after Stone was convicted of witness tampering and lying to federal investigators.

He fought to preserve Southern Civil War monuments and decried efforts to ban the Confederate Battle Flag. He echoed Nixon's "law and order" rallying cry in defending police against charges of brutality against Black Americans. He excused white supremacists after they clashed with civil rights advocates in Virginia, declaring that there were "very fine people on both sides."

Just as George Wallace had stood in the schoolhouse door to defend segregation, Trump stood on the stops of the White House to defend white America against those who dared to say that Black lives mattered.

But there was a difference between Wallace and Trump.

Wallace apologized for his racist past at the age of 75, while Trump at age 74 apologized for nothing as he sat in the White House. Wallace's stand in the schoolhouse door was symbolic: He stepped aside when the Alabama National Guard showed up to escort two black students inside. Trump, by contrast, refuses to ever step aside. Not in the face of criticism, not even in the aftermath of a convincing election defeat.

To evangelicals whose motto has long been "no compromise," he's just the kind of hero they've always envisioned.

STEPHEN H. PROVOST

"It is unpatriotic not to tell the truth, whether about the president or anyone else."

Theodore Roosevelt,
26th president of the United States

Lost Causes

One of Donald Trump's biggest symbolic causes has been his steadfast opposition to athletes kneeling during the national anthem. It didn't matter that kneeling was actually the brainchild of a former Green Beret named Nate Boyer — who suggested it as an alternative after NFL player Colin Kaepernick remained seated during the anthem to protest police brutality.

Kaepernick took Boyer up on that suggestion. It seemed like a reasonable compromise that allowed the quarterback to make a statement and, at the same time, preserve respect. After all, kneeling was a sign of deference, wasn't it?

Trump wasn't having any of it, though. Even with the change, he complained that Kaepernick was disrespecting both the flag and those who had served.

No compromise.

Kaepernick's point, of course, had nothing to do with the flag or veterans. It was all about protesting the kind of racial violence that ultimately led to the death of George Floyd, who would be killed in police custody in 2020.

He was far from the first. Indeed, Floyd's death was merely the most visible example of police using lethal force against African Americans. Statistics showed that Blacks were 2.8 times more likely to die in custody than whites, and that Black victims were more likely to be unarmed. But as the video of Floyd being choked to death would prove, visual images are far more effective in reaching an audience than statistics — especially in front of a national audience.

Trump, the former star of a TV reality show, knew this, too. Later on, he would use this knowledge to maximum effect himself. He would counter statistics that showed millions of Americans had gotten sick from coronavirus with images of packed political rallies. He would pressure colleges to play football and schools to reopen. He would rip off his facemask defiantly on his return from the hospital after being treated for the virus.

When athletes knelt for the anthem, he responded with images of the American flag. Republicans had succeeded in hijacking the concept of "patriotism" by draping themselves in the flag long before Trump came along; he simply exploited it by taking it to another level.

For all his talk about patriotism and the flag, it might seem odd that Trump should also defend the flag of a short-lived breakaway republic that fought a bloody war with the United States. More than 600,000 people died in the Civil War: a rebellion against the United States and the president Trump has praised repeatedly, Abraham Lincoln.

It would seem like a blatant contradiction.

But only if you view Trump's opposition to the practice of kneeling as all about the flag.

Not So Contradictory

What if he knew full well that it was meant as a protest against racism and police brutality? And what if part of the reason he opposed Kaepernick's action was an implicit nod toward racism?

Consider: Trump explicitly opposed the Black Lives Matter movement, which was formed in response to police violence against Black Americans. The flag didn't motivate his opposition; neither did respect for U.S. veterans. But that opposition did fit right into his "law and order" message which backed police against Black protesters. To Trump, the protesters were rioters and looters, while the police were white knights standing in the breach between innocent citizens and bloody chaos.

The reality was much more complicated.

Yes, there was rioting and looting, but TV coverage, which focuses on the sensational, made it seem far worse than it was. And most of what did occur was the work of outsiders and opportunists, not the protesters themselves.

Police, meanwhile, weren't all good guys out to keep the peace and save the day. Some were quite the opposite. After a white teenager named Kyle Rittenhouse shot three people (killing two of them) on the streets of Kenosha, Wis., he walked right past police patrols with his hands — and gun — raised in the air.

They did nothing to stop him.

Were they distracted? Incompetent? Complicit? It's impossible to tell.

But a 2006 FBI report warned that white racists were continuing a historic pattern of infiltrating law enforcement, which included both "strategic infiltration by organized groups" and independent efforts by racist sympathizers.

A counter-terrorism guide in 2015 identified active links between police and white supremacists, as well as so-called "militia" extremists and "sovereign citizen" movements.

Open-carry laws, such as the one that allowed Kyle Rittenhouse to tote his rifle on the streets of Kenosha, have increased both the boldness and visibility of these movements. One of them hatched a brazen plot to kidnap the Michigan Gov. Gretchen Whitmer, with backup plans for an armed invasion of the statehouse.

What did law enforcement do?

One Michigan sheriff seemed to support at least the motive behind the plot, stating that "a lot of people are angry with the governor and want her arrested." He then questioned whether the plot was, in fact, a plan to abduct Whitmer — or, rather, make a citizens' arrest.

Trump himself was similarly ambivalent, saying "maybe it was a problem, maybe it wasn't."

The comment was reminiscent of his declaration that there were "very fine people on both sides" of the deadly Charlottesville protests involving white supremacists.

Coupled with Trump's own criticism of Whitmer, his comments seemed to give the militia group behind the plot a pass. The president preferred to focus on Islamic terrorists, even though their attacks on U.S. soil over the years have been fewer and far less deadly than those launched by white supremacists.

These actions by Trump, together with his efforts to suppress or throw out votes by Black citizens in areas such as Detroit, illustrate that he endorses the goal of the old Confederacy: to support a white ruling class by preserving its historic economic and cultural dominance.

Many white Americans who consider themselves "patriots" share this objective, which explains why American and Confederate flags fly side-by-side on many private properties, especially in the South.

In many cases, they also identify themselves as Christians and aim to reclaim the United States as a "Christian nation." Extremist groups like the Ku Klux Klan and the Christian Identity movement have long emphasized their ties to Christianity. Most evangelicals aren't part of such radical groups, and most would disavow their methods. But that doesn't mean they don't share some of their goals, such as opposing same-sex marriage and "saving Christmas" from secular incursions.

Liberal Missteps

Many liberals and progressives, in their efforts in promoting diversity and inclusion, have alienated white Christians who might have been sympathetic to their cause with broad-brush statements that stigmatize entire groups.

Language matters.

Calls to "defund" (rather than *reform*) the police led to defensiveness among supporters of law enforcement. They created the kind of binary dynamic that extremists thrive on exploiting: "Either you're with us or against us." Either black lives matter or blue lives do. There is no in-between.

This kind of self-sabotage — responding to extremist views and prejudice with exaggerated language and stereotyping — can undermine opposition to bigotry by forcing people to make what they see as an unfair choice. Or to feel guilty about their own identity.

This false guilt often leads to defensiveness rather than self-examination, which defeats the purpose and can alienate potential allies. It's also the product of flawed reasoning.

Evangelical churches aren't merely "fronts" for white racism or Trump supporters. Remember, between one-fifth and one-quarter of white evangelicals didn't vote for Trump and don't support his character and/or his agenda. It's more accurate to say that such churches are often *favored by* racists and Trump supporters. Sometimes, but not always, they're controlled by them, too. But that doesn't make white evangelical Christianity synonymous with racism.

The same principle goes for law enforcement. There's no question that white supremacists have targeted police and sheriff's departments as a means of seizing power. The significance of this should not be understated, and we shouldn't be distracted from the dangers it poses by focusing instead on Islamic extremism. But we also shouldn't assert that law enforcement is merely a puppet of white racists.

It's possible for systemic, baked-in bigotry and racism to be present in an institution without indicting every police officer who wears a badge or every evangelical Christian who goes to church on Sunday.

That being said, there's no question that Trump's winks, nods, dog whistles, and shout-outs have emboldened the more extreme elements within those groups. And because members of insular "bubble" groups tend to become more extreme whatever their beliefs, enabling these views creates a danger that radicalism will spread further in churches, police departments, and other conservative groups. You can see it happening in Congress, where pundits have been mystified that Republicans had gone along with Trump's extreme, offensive, and potentially illegal actions.

They shouldn't be.

Congress itself is an insular institution, shielded from the "real world" from its inside-the-Beltway mentality. But more than this, the people Washington lawmakers represent live in their own insular bubbles, as well. And they're becoming more extreme.

Lawmakers have only themselves to thank (or blame) for this phenomenon. Over the years, they've systematically created and fortified political bubbles via gerrymandering: the practice of creating "safe" districts to ensure incumbents are re-elected.

These districts are drawn in such a way that large numbers of Democrats and liberals are grouped together, while Republicans and conservatives find themselves dominating other districts. As with any other bubble, the people in these districts reinforce each other's views, with liberals becoming more liberal and conservatives more conservative. The result is that moderate voices become fewer and weaker, with representatives reflecting increasingly polarized views.

Gridlock ensues, nothing gets done, and frustrated voters become increasingly open to taking extreme actions to get things done — even if it means undermining long-established norms and systems to do so.

Thus is tribal politics the gateway to tyranny.

In such an atmosphere, people in the minority feel like victims. And when someone like Trump comes along and empowers their victimhood with his own personal grievances, he can create a powerful and tenacious grip on them — to the point that they think their own identity is threatened if he loses.

When South Carolina Sen. Lindsey Graham (once a fierce Trump critic) was asked why he was insinuating himself into Georgia's presidential vote audit, he answered succinctly, "Because the future of the country is at stake."

Could bubble-based extremism be behind Graham's about-face on Trump and drift toward extremism?

You be the judge.

Causes Lost and Found

The Confederacy lasted barely four years, but the "Lost Cause" narrative has endured for more than a century and a half. It's an attempt to resolve the cognitive dissonance between a sentimental attachment to the antebellum South and the reality of the Confederacy's defeat in the Civil War.

The narrative is one of victimhood and grievance that drives its proponents to continue the fight, even though the war has been lost. It's a form of denial that can result in a stubborn refusal to accept the facts. And, sometimes, that stubbornness can actually *change* the facts.

Since the Civil War, for example, "Lost Cause" champions have succeeded in destroying Reconstruction — a government-backed effort to impose racial equality on the postwar South. In its aftermath, they instituted poll taxes and literacy tests to keep Black southerners from voting. They replaced slavery with segregation and Jim Crow. They erected monuments to fallen heroes like Jefferson Davis and Robert E. Lee, and they continued to fly the Confederate battle flag.

Yes, that's the *battle* flag. The starred blue "X" on a red field wasn't the national flag of the Confederacy (which was known as the "Stars and Bars"), it was in fact a call to arms. Back then, it meant fighting for the Confederacy; today some see it as an emblem of Southern pride, even it's also a symbol of slavery that's often displayed by white supremacist groups.

But the Confederacy isn't the only "lost cause." The phrase can apply to any ill-fated campaign by true believers who yet can't accept the reality of their own defeat.

As the United States grows more diverse, the white majority narrative is becoming a "lost cause" in its own right. As of 2019, the share of non-Hispanic white U.S. residents had dropped to barely 60% — down from 87.5% in 1950. Suburbs were increasingly integrated, and in states such as California, non-Hispanic whites were already in the minority: In the Golden State, they'd fallen below 37%.

White evangelical Christians have seen a similar decline, from 21% as recently in 2010 to 15% by the end of the decade. One article even declared that "White Christian America ended in the 2010s," the same decade that saw the re-election of the first Black president.

But the lost-causers struck back by electing one of their own in 2016: Donald Trump.

Trump's reaction to his defeat in the 2020 election was to create an alternate reality that rivaled the Confederacy's lost-cause narrative in outrageousness and tenacity. He declared himself the rightful winner, despite universal evidence to the contrary. He refused to concede after losing by 6 million votes. He demanded recount after recount, and pushed state legislators to toss out the vote entirely. He targeted the court of public opinion after losing in actual courts. It was all, in fact, hopeless. A lost cause. But like the postwar South, Trump hoped to snatch victory from the arms of defeat simply by willing it to be so.

What do white supremacy — the Confederacy's defining philosophy — white evangelical Christianity, and Donald Trump have in common?

They're all losing their grip on America, and they're all desperate to somehow keep that from happening.

"Do you know what we call opinion in the absence of evidence? We call it prejudice."

Michael Crichton,
bestselling author, filmmaker

STEPHEN H. PROVOST

Hearing is Believing

"Faith comes by hearing, and hearing by the word of God."

So wrote Paul of Tarsus in his letter to the Romans, but it wasn't quite that simple. The message Paul was spreading seemed hard to believe. A man named Jesus had risen from the dead? Seriously? Sure, there were myths about gods who'd risen from the dead, but he was talking about a real person who'd lived and died in the past few years.

There wasn't any good forensic evidence that it had happened. The best that could be said was that he'd been buried, his body had vanished (even though it had been placed under guard), and a few people claimed to have seen him afterward. Unfortunately, though, this Jesus wasn't around anymore, so no one could ask him about it.

Believing a story like that must have seemed like a pretty tall order at the time, yet it caught on, and today, more than 2 billion people accept it — nearly a third of the world's population. They don't believe it based on evidence, but based on faith.

The problem with faith, regardless of whether you're talking about religion or anything else, is how to decide where to place it. Some people put their faith in something because the evidence supports it. Others believe because they trust the source of the information, even if they can't check it out themselves. Still others believe because they want to believe: The story is, on some level, so appealing that they decide it's better to believe than not to do so. And then there are those who believe out of the fear that, if they don't, something bad will happen.

Augustine put his own faith in the last of these reasons: The threat of force was the surest way to "compel them to come in." Blaise Pascal argued that it was better to believe that God exists — and take a chance on receiving infinite rewards if he does — than to risk an eternity in hell by believing he didn't. If you believe in God and you're wrong, Pascal argued, you don't have nearly as much to lose.

None of that had anything to do with evidence, but rather with a simple principle of reward vs. punishment. And, of course, it didn't take into account other possibilities: That a different god might exist instead, for example, who might offer similar rewards for faith and punishments for refusing to believe in *him*. Or her.

The point is that, in the absence of

evidence, you've got to come up with another basis for believing something — if, in fact, you wish to believe.

That's where conspiracy theories come in. To ancient skeptics, the story of Jesus might have sounded very much like a conspiracy theory. One explanation, contained in the Gospel of Matthew, was that the guards had fallen asleep and Jesus' disciples had stolen his body from the tomb. Or maybe, others have suggested, Jesus actually survived the crucifixion and somehow managed to wander out of the cave.

Some have dismissed these ideas as implausible, while others have responded that anything's more plausible than someone rising from the dead.

Ultimately, the truth of the matter can't be determined based on evidence. All the witnesses are long dead, and there was no police tape to keep the "scene of the crime" from getting contaminated in the first century. Absent such evidence, any conclusion — either way — is based on faith (or the lack thereof).

You can't say the same thing about modern conspiracy theories: There's enough evidence to debunk most of them. But that hasn't stopped them from spreading, because some people believe things in spite of the evidence, not for any lack of it.

Some fall into the category of believing what they want to believe. Others believe what they're *told* to believe by sources they trust, either because they think they'll be rewarded for their faith or punished if they lack it.

For such people, everything takes the form of Pascal's Wager.

Pros and Conspiracies

Donald Trump, the former casino owner, knows all about wagering. He also practices a version of reward and punishment that reflects the alternatives presented in Christian theology pretty closely. Eternal bliss or everlasting torment: The choice is yours.

Trump routinely promises the biggest and the best rewards (even if he can't produce them) on the one hand, while at the same time bullying his enemies and punching back "ten times harder" if he's attacked. He promises his supporters the closest thing to heaven in exchange for their loyalty and vows to put his enemies through a version of hell on earth — on Twitter and in court.

It makes sense, therefore, that Trump also knows a lot about conspiracy theories. He hatches them, repeats them, and insists that his followers parrot them. Or else.

In the absence of proof, or in the face of evidence to the contrary, Trump knows two things will make a conspiracy theory stick: repeating it often enough, and getting enough people to buy in. As a media figure and, later, as president, Trump had a built-in megaphone to repeat whatever B.S. happened to benefit him. And as his exposure grew, more and more people supported his efforts.

His first and still most famous conspiracy theory was the absurd notion that Barack Obama had been born in Kenya, which would have made him ineligible to serve as president. Obama refuted it, even producing his official birth certificate to debunk it. But the notion stuck because Trump pushed it so hard, and many people still believe it today.

After he won the 2016 election in the Electoral College, Trump insisted he'd won the popular vote as well, even though the numbers said otherwise. He insisted his inauguration had drawn more people than any other president's, despite photographic evidence to the contrary.

After the 2020 election, which he lost by something like 6 million votes, he insisted — again without evidence — that the election had been stolen, and withheld any concession, even though he lost more convincingly than he'd won four years earlier.

Long after votes were cast, Trump

remained defiant, even though nearly all of his legal challenges were failing and every recount confirmed he'd lost.

"I concede NOTHING!" Trump tweeted. "This was a RIGGED ELECTION!"

There was nothing to substantiate any of this, and even Twitter itself flagged Trump's message with a notice that his claim was disputed and a link to a statement from election experts calling voter fraud of any kind "exceedingly rare."

The fact that Trump was making his charges without evidence mystified some and confounded others, but it was exactly what we should have expected from him.

When the head of his own election security agency called it "the most secure in American history," Trump fired him on Twitter, producing a laundry list of accusations ranging from votes cast by dead people to machines that inexplicably changed votes from him to Joe Biden.

Without evidence.

He sent celebrity lawyer Rudy Giuliani into court to lay out his argument for voter fraud in Pennsylvania. But Giuliani — a former New York City mayor who hadn't argued a before a trial judge in decades — made broad accusations.

Again, without evidence.

Giuliani relied more on colorful language and demanded that the court take extreme action even though, by his own admission, he wasn't even alleging fraud.

"You're asking this court to invalidate more than 6.8 million votes, thereby disenfranchising every single voter in the commonwealth," the judge said. "Can you tell me how this result can possibly be justified?"

Giuliani responded that the remedy was "draconian because the conduct was egregious."

If the judge ruled against him, he said, he would appeal. And when that happened, Trump vowed to take it all the way to the Supreme Court. His campaign, meanwhile, was pursuing court cases in other states, as well, even though there was no evidence of widespread problems there, either.

After a while, it started to seem like a game of whack-a-mole, with Trump making baseless charges, only to either withdraw them or have them rejected out of hand by the courts, then start all over again. He did win one case in Pennsylvania, but it didn't involve anywhere near enough votes to affect the outcome.

But he wasn't, in the main, making his case to judges. He was staging a reality-show version of political theater meant to be consumed by his fervent supporters.

Trump's flurry of baseless lawsuits reinforced the image he'd built for himself as a fighter: an image his core supporters love, regardless of the outcome. To the outside world, he looked more like Don Quixote than anything else, sharing his first name in common with the windmill-tilting dreamer. But within the bubble he'd helped build around his supporters, he was David fighting Goliath.

There was simply nothing to support Trump's claims of election fraud, any more than there'd been anything to back his contention that Obama had been born in Kenya. It was, plain and simple, pure fantasy.

Yet people in Trump bubble believed them.

Confidence Game

After the election, large numbers of people descended upon Washington, D.C., to protest the results, convinced that Trump had won. Based on... well, probably just because they wanted it to be true, which is apparently the same reason Trump clung to his fanciful assertion. The man who promised his followers they'd always be winning had just lost, yet he refused to acknowledge it.

For one thing, he hates to lose, and refuses to even admit the possibility as a means of protecting his overblown yet extremely fragile ego. But there's a broader goal — and consequence — to his extreme confidence, even in the face of the facts.

It's contagious.

Studies have shown that people exposed to overconfidence by someone in their own social group tend to become overconfident themselves. So if Trump projects a high level of certainty that he's won an election (even though the numbers make it clear he hasn't), his supporters are likely to pick up on it and amplify it.

Since faith is a form of confidence, it can be contagious, too. Stories of martyrs who refused to renounce their faith, even as they faced death, became sources of inspiration to early Christians. These stories, in turn, bolstered the faith of those who heard them. If they had been so certain that a reward awaited them in the next life, who was anyone to argue?

Unwavering expressions of certainty play on the desire for security, offering reassurance that can offset objections based on facts — especially if those facts change over time. For instance, Trump began claiming the 2020 election was rigged months before the first votes were even cast, and held firm to this assessment when the election was over. The vote totals themselves, however, changed over the course of several days as ballots were counted, shifting mostly away from Trump and toward Joe Biden as time went on.

It was easy for Trump's supporters to believe his stubborn insistence that the election was rigged when they contrasted it with vote totals that changed quickly over the course of just a few days.

Similarly, Trump's steady confidence that the coronavirus would soon be under control contrasted sharply with infection rates that rose, then fell, then spiked again, and with changing guidance from officials who first told the public not to wear masks, then switched gears and said it was essential.

The experts' ultimate guidance was correct, but Trump used the fact that they'd changed their tune to dismiss *anything* they might say. And again, his followers believed him.

But why should Trump's consistency count for so much in these cases, when — as pointed out earlier — he often changes gears himself, for no apparent reason, in other situations? Why should his supporters give him credit for being consistent on the one hand, and excuse his erratic behavior on the other?

For two reasons. First, he's their leader, a godlike figure who gets credit for providing a steady hand in times of crisis and is above reproach when things go wrong. Secondly, in both cases, he's telling people what he wants them to believe. That's the source of their faith, not any evidence. In the case of the election, they want to believe he's won. In the case of the coronavirus, they want to believe it will just "go away" like "a miracle."

Miracles, of course, are exceptions to the natural order.

They're chaotic by nature.

In being confident that a miracle will occur, Trump is operating in exactly the opposite way science does. Science is a process that uses doubt to arrive at factual conclusions. Scientists begin with a hypothesis and the suspicion that it might be *wrong*. Then they say, "Prove it to me." They test the hypothesis, and if it doesn't work, they learn from their mistakes, come up with a new hypothesis (or refine the old one) and try again. They repeat this process until they find something that *does* work.

Religious faith begins with not just the assumption, but the conviction, that something works. If it appears to come up short, believers ignore any shortcomings and try the same thing again. And again. And again. And they proclaim even their failures successful because they can't possibly be otherwise.

Whereas science begins with doubt, faith proceeds from certainty. I say "proceeds," but it doesn't really go anywhere, because it knows the answer before it starts. Whether that answer is factual or not is immaterial. What matters — all that matters — is faith.

This is precisely Trump's way of dealing with the world. As he rose to power, then maintained it, pundits scratched their head, asking, "Why does this work?" Here was a man who projected supreme confidence, who began with the assumption that he knew everything, and who refused to apologize if things went wrong. Or even acknowledge that they *had* gone wrong. A man who never learned from his mistakes because he denied he'd ever made any — that he even *could* make any.

In Trump's world, any apparent mistakes are simply false accusations from enemies who are intent on bringing him down. They're "fake news." Viruses and election defeats are all just hoaxes perpetrated by socialists, blue-state Democrat mayors, the "lamestream" media, and anyone else who dares question Trump's word.

No one who has seen a televangelist operate should be scratching their head, because Trump is using the same paradigm: ignorance, supreme confidence, and victimhood. It's the perfect formula for winning over white evangelicals, and it has worked like a charm.

That confidence worked just as well for Trump when he found himself embroiled in an actual conspiracy of his own. He used the same method to push back against it as he had when he'd pushed his own conspiracy theories: He created an alternative reality, and he stuck to it.

There was no doubt he'd spoken to the president of Ukraine on the phone. There were official records of what the two men had said. Vladimir Zelensky told Trump he wanted to buy defensive missiles from the United States. But Trump responded by appearing to place an implicit condition on the sale. His words sounded like something out of a mob negotiation: "I'd like you to do us a favor, though."

The favor? Looking into unfounded allegations against the son of Trump's most likely opponent in the 2020 election — the man who ultimately beat him.

True to form, when news of the call came to light, Trump didn't apologize or admit he'd done anything wrong. He didn't try to deny he'd said what had been reported. (Since there was a record of it, that wouldn't have been a good option.) Instead of saying he'd misspoken or been misunderstood, he went in the opposite direction: He called it a "perfect" phone call.

Repeatedly.

Through the power of his office and the audacity of his certitude, he created a false narrative that left people second-guessing themselves rather than him: a strategy known as gaslighting.

He brazenly set out to bamboozle the entire country.

And it worked. Although he was impeached for his actions, he was acquitted by a friendly Republican Senate.

WhoAnon?

Trump even uses conspiracy theories to his advantage when they pop up independently of him — no matter how absurd they might seem. Take, for instance, the accusations spread by QAnon: that Trump himself is secretly fighting against a ring of Satan-worshipping pedophiles engaged in a worldwide six-trafficking operation.

When questioned about the group, Trump took pleasure in the fact that "they like me very much," but claimed to know very little about them. Of course, this would fit with the cabal's narrative that Trump was fighting these devil worshippers behind the scenes, so of course he would feign ignorance even though he knew exactly what was going on. Nod, nod. Wink, wink.

That's one thing about conspiracy theories: they're *theories* — or, rather, fantasies. There's nothing to them, but they're often so shrouded in mystery that it's hard to disprove them. Frequently, it's even impossible to trace their origins, so you can't discredit their sources, either.

Who is "Q"?

Does such a person even exist? It's impossible to say.

What is clear, however, is that accusations are nothing new. The only thing that's changed is who's being accused.

Accusations of witchcraft and heresy were the conspiracy theories of choice in the medieval world. They were hard to disprove and could be devastating because the stakes were so high: You were typically presumed at the outset, and you could wind up dead based on allegations alone.

If you had a grudge against someone, the best way to exact revenge (and to get them out of the way) was to accuse the person of a crime against the church.

The most famous cases occurred, of course, during the witch crazy of 1692 and '93 in Salem,

Mass. More than 200 people were accused, 20 were executed, and five others died in jail.

None were witches.

Accusations of witchcraft were based on envy and malice rather than evidence.

In fact, the entire craze was built on a feud between the area's two most prominent families. And the dynamics parallel both the Civil War era and the polarized politics of our modern age.

Then, as now, a rift emerged between urban and rural interests, led by two prominent families, which threatened to tear Salem in two. The area's richest family, the Porters, made their fortune as harbor merchants; their closest rivals, the Putnams lived inland and had accumulated their wealth through farming.

The more devout Putnams and their circle wanted to form their own community, independent of the coastal Salem Town. Essentially, they wanted to secede. The Town refused.

In a compromise of sorts, the farming group

was granted permission hiring their own minister, one Samuel Parris.

But the town ultimately decided to stop paying him, and that's when things got ugly. Parris' daughter and her cousin accused his slave girl of witchcraft. It was a quintessential example of scapegoating: Tituba wasn't just a slave, but also an immigrant and person of color, likely from South America or Barbados. Her husband was a Native American.

The witchcraft conspiracy grew from there, fueled by a combination of fear and anger. It had all the components of future conflicts:

- Prejudice
- Religious justification
- An urban-rural divide
- Economic friction
- Paranoia/conspiracy theories

Trump's approach to seizing and maintaining power rested on these same pillars. His conspiracy theory in the 2020 election? Big-city Democrats were trying to steal the election.

He attempted to use this as a justification to disenfranchise large numbers of voters in major cities, a large percentage of whom were Black. When he took these cases to court, he lost, even before friendly judges, because U.S. courts require evidence to rule in someone's favor — and Trump had none.

But the very lack of evidence that stymied him in the courts worked in his favor when he appealed to his supporters. Unlike judges, who'd taken an oath of impartiality, they were already predisposed to believe him. And his promises that he'd reveal the truth "soon" invited them to have faith... so they could receive a dose of dopamine.

He accused others of spreading hoaxes, even though he was the one doing so. He charged that his opponents were trying to game the system, which is exactly what he was trying to do. And he claimed to be the target of a "witch hunt," when he was the one intent on ruining his enemies' reputations.

QAnon believers worked the same way:

relying on faith and dangled-carrot promises to keep interest high, while making outlandish claims against their opponents, and failing to back them up with evidence.

Satanic Panics

Although QAnon bears a clear resemblance to the Salem witch trials, a far closer and more recent parallel exists: the "satanic panic" of the 1980s.

It's all but forgotten now, but many of the same people who promoted this set of conspiracies — like televangelists and right-wing conspiracy monger Geraldo Rivera (remember Al Capone's vault?) — remain active today.

The movement was spearheaded, not surprisingly, by Moral Majority types who enlisted the help of Tipper Gore and other Washington wives to combat violent and suggestive lyrics in popular music. But Gore's efforts, through her group, the Parents Music

Resource Center, were just the tip of the iceberg.

The lyrics were there for everyone to see, and so was a Senate hearing that pitted the PMRC against musicians as diverse as John Denver, Frank Zappa, and Dee Snider of Twisted Sister. Each of them argued against placing warning labels on CDs and records, condemning the process as a form of censorship. But the music industry had already agreed to the labels *before* the hearing took place, so the die had been cast.

Whatever one's opinions about the PMRC labels, they weren't the worst thing to come out of the assault on popular music. Alongside the labeling campaign, evangelical leaders pushed more sinister conspiracy theories. Some musicians, they alleged, were intentionally placing hidden messages in their music. When played backward, these messages supposedly encouraged devil worship, suicide, and other destructive behavior.

Band names were interpreted as code

words, too. KISS was said to stand for Kids, Knights, or Kings in Satan's Service. AC/DC supposedly was shorthand for Anti-Christ/Devil's Child. There wasn't an iota of truth to any of it, but song titles like "Highway to Hell," "Hotter Than Hell," "Night Prowler," and "Suicide Solution" lent credence to the charges — at least in the minds of paranoid suburban white parents, who feared their children were being secretly indoctrinated into a satanic cult.

As with QAnon, concern for the safety of children was the satanic panic's main appeal. Parents and prosecutors sued rock acts like Ozzy Osbourne, AC/DC, and Judas Priest, charging that messages in their music had led young people to commit suicide or murder.

Rivera (later a Trump supporter) hosted an NBC special report titled *Devil Worship: Exposing Satan's Underground*, in which he stoked suburban fears by alleging that a "secret network" of more than a million Satanists were broadcasting covert messages via heavy metal music.

No one would have mistaken KISS or Ozzy Osbourn for pillars of virtue. But that didn't mean they were engaged in some nefarious plot. Most of them were too busy with sex, drugs, and rock 'n' roll to hatch such devious schemes, even if they'd wanted to. And there's no indication they did.

But the conspiracy charges didn't end with obvious targets like debauched rock stars. The people behind the growing craze soon expanded their web to ensnare child-care workers, as well.

Claims began to surface in several preschools, few if any of which were ever proven.

Most famously, it was alleged that 48 children at the McMartin Preschool in Southern California had been sexually abused in bizarre satanic rituals, and prosecutors considered them credible enough to bring to 321 criminal charges.

None of them stuck.

Prosecutors spent seven years and spent $15 million in government money trying to prove their case, but they came up empty, producing zero convictions. One teacher at the preschool spent five years behind bars before finally being exonerated and released.

No widespread satanic cult was ever uncovered, and most of the accusations turned out to have been based on coerced testimony and manufactured "memories" of events that had never occurred.

But at the height of the craze — and this is the crucial point — 87% of those responding to a TV poll said they believed the defendants were guilty.

Conspiracy theories work. They may not convince judges, but in the court of public opinion, they can be pure gold for those seeking to profit from the fear they induce. And no fear is more powerful than the fear among parents that their kids are in danger.

In light of this, it's no surprise that QAnon,

like the satanic panic, stokes just this kind of fear. Once again, a mysterious devil-worshipping cabal is supposedly behind it all, and once again, children are the targets.

As the author of Ecclesiastes once wrote, there's nothing new under the sun.

"Baseless victimhood is usually the last stage before outright aggression."

Stefan Molyneux,
white supremacist

STEPHEN H. PROVOST

Martyr Don

It might seem odd that someone who stakes his reputation on winning should so consistently try to play the victim, but that's what Donald Trump has done. And, when you think about it, it makes perfect sense.

Victimhood gives you the perfect excuse for failure, because failure is never your fault. Someone else is always to blame. As long as you've got a scapegoat, you can deflect attention off your own shortcomings.

Besides, if you cast yourself as a victim, you put pressure on others to sympathize with you. This is especially true in today's society, where blaming the victim is considered cruel and shameful.

Clinical psychologist David J. Ley put it this way in Psychology Today: "For many years, victims have been bullied, shamed, and blamed, which worsens the effects of their experience. Unfortunately, in a swing to the opposite side, victimhood has now become a protected class in our society..."

Ley points out that alleged victims often receive "financial support and other secondary gains" as the result of proclaiming their victimhood.

"Why would people loudly and publicly proclaim themselves as victims?" Ley asks. "Perhaps a better question, based upon the level of secondary gain, attention, protection, and support received by these people, is why wouldn't they? ... Why are we surprised when people are exaggerating, using, or downright lying, about victimization?"

Turning the Tables

The dynamic was on public display at the Supreme Court confirmation hearings for Brent Kavanaugh, who faced accusations from Christine Blasey Ford that he had groped and tried to undress her during high school in the 1980s.

Ford was a respected professor whose testimony seemed sincere and credible. Kavanaugh, a Trump nominee, was a respected judge being considered for the highest court in the nation. But the issue didn't come down to sincerity or credibility, or even evidence. It came down to a single factor:

Victimhood.

Ford would seem to have been the victim in the case, and her supporters affirmed her in this status. When it came time, however, for Kavanaugh to defend himself, he flipped the script.

Instead of presenting evidence to rebut his accuser, he cast *himself* as the true victim.

In his opening statement, he cast doubt on the proceedings themselves, declaring that "this confirmation process has become a national disgrace." The language and the strategy were both pure Trump — who revels in dismissing anything he doesn't like as a "disgrace," and who would seek to delegitimize the 2020 election in much the same way Kavanaugh called the Senate hearings into question.

"This is a circus," he said angrily, first expressing righteous indignation and then becoming choked up.

Kavanaugh, who had been nominated for a nonpartisan position, framed opposition to his confirmation in highly partisan terms: as "a calculated and orchestrated political hit, fueled with apparent pent-up anger about President Trump and the 2016 election."

With the help of a Republican Senate majority, Kavanaugh's victimhood won the day.

Whether Kavanaugh was guilty of the allegations against him became immaterial, because he didn't use reason to argue against them, as one might expect from a candidate for the high court.

Instead, he appealed to emotion.

Indeed, by the standards of reason, his defense was all over the map:

Ford's accusation was old — it "dated back more than 36 years." Kavanaugh admitted he was "not perfect in those days," partying and drinking beer. The charges constituted "character assassination," and if they were allowed to stand, it would discourage competent people of all political persuasions from serving their country.

None of this constituted evidence that refuted Ford's allegation.

Granted, it's difficult to prove a negative. That's why Kavanaugh's supporters — including Trump — pointed to a presumption of innocence in criminal courts. (Even though the Senate hearing was not a criminal proceeding.)

Kavanaugh himself was careful to apply the same presumption of innocence to Ford: He didn't accuse her of defaming him, and even said he wasn't questioning that Ford might have been assaulted. "But," he insisted. "I have never done this."

He then went on to invoke a different kind of innocence: the innocence of his own 10-year-old daughter in suggesting they should pray for Ford. But not for those who believed her, who were guilty of "grotesque" politically motivated "character assassination."

It was a masterful defense, appealing to religion in an effort to depict Kavanaugh's daughter (and Kavanaugh himself, by association) as bestowing forgiveness on a poor, misguided woman who thought she was a victim.

But she wasn't. Kavanaugh was the one who had been wronged (or so he claimed), and his emotional defense was a potent example of the power of victimhood.

Trump might have done well to take notes, but on second thought, he didn't need to: He'd been playing the victim himself for years by the time Kavanaugh made his defense.

So had evangelical leaders.

They'd crafted a narrative in which they, the "moral majority," were under siege from a godless horde intent on thwarting their righteous goal of establishing the kingdom of God on earth. Traditional values were being cast aside. Interracial and gay marriage, feminism, and prohibitions on prayer in public schools were undermining the "family values" that had made America great.

When Trump vowed to make it great again, he was speaking their language: the language of victimhood. Many have wondered how blue-collar workers who attend church faithfully and condemn adultery could support a billionaire playboy known for womanizing who's seldom seen in church. What could they possibly have in common?

The answer is their shared sense of entitlement and, conversely, grievance and victimhood.

The most revered figures in Christian history are martyrs: Men and women unjustly condemned for their faith. That a jet-setting golf course owner should cast himself, successfully, as a modern martyr (figuratively speaking) in the minds of the men and women with whom he has virtually nothing else in common speaks to the power of victimhood.

Even when that victimhood is false.

Even when the "hoaxes" aren't hoaxes and the "fake news" is real.

Welcome to 1984.

"We're the only winners.
The players don't stand a
chance."

Sam "Ace" Rothstein,
fictional gambling handicapper in *Casino*

STEPHEN H. PROVOST

The House Always Wins

Donald Trump had toyed with the idea of running for president several times before, floating the possibility for the first time in 1988. But he'd never pulled the trigger, because the time had never been right.

In 2015, it finally was.

Trump had spent a lifetime creating his own alternate reality, and the Republican Party — with the help of Rush Limbaugh, Fox News, and the Tea Party — was doing the same thing.

All he had to do was to hijack *that* reality and subsume it to his massive ego, and he'd have pulled off the coup of the century.

In the end, that's exactly what he did.

At first glance, Trump would seem like the last person you'd expect to be a hero to Christians. His image as a rule-breaker, whether it came to business deals or marriage contracts, would seem to make him the antithesis of Christian values.

Critics viewed evangelicals' embrace of Trump with chagrin and bemusement. How could any Christian possibly choose such an amoral person as their champion?

But remember, we aren't talking about morals. We're talking about goals and how to achieve them. When viewed in this light, the evangelical church's affinity for Trump is easily understood.

Like Augustine, they view Trump as a means to an end. The bishop from Hippo had exchanged appeals to reason for the use of force in seeking to convert ancient "heathens" to the Christian faith. He'd abandoned his principles to achieve his goals.

Trump has repeatedly done the same.

Moreover, he understands the dynamic of faith, as defined by evangelicals — and, more specifically, by prosperity preachers. He spent two decades running casinos, and any casino owner understands how the game is played: Board up the windows and tear down the clocks to keep your customers in a bubble. Then keep the dopamine (and the cash) flowing. They get a kick out of gambling, but the casino is playing them, because the house always wins.

"People think I'm a gambler," Trump once said. "I've never gambled in my life. To me, a gambler is someone who plays slot machines. I prefer to own slot machines. It's a very good business being the house."

Just like it's very good business being the church. Churches don't pay taxes, and Trump refuses to disclose his, bragging that he doesn't pay much, either, because he knows how to work the system.

Why did Trump cling so desperately to power long after it was clear that he'd lost the 2020 presidential election? The answer is simple: To him, the president was the house. Since the house always wins, it was inconceivable to him that he could have possibly lost. And, more crucially, he didn't want to give up the advantage of being the house.

The power it entailed.

The ability to rake in cash through connections and transactional "deals."

The immunity from prosecution that enabled him to keep right on breaking the rules. Because, as any casino operator knows, the house *makes* the rules: It makes the odds and dictates how (un)likely you are to win if you're playing the slots.

If you go to Vegas, you might see various casinos advertise the "loosest slots in town." They're competing with one another to draw you in. But if one person owned all the casinos, there'd be no need for that kind of competition. The only thing you'd have to worry about would be making it too difficult to win. You wouldn't want players to stop playing. (But even this isn't a very big worry when you're dealing with dopamine-driven gamblers.)

As the president of the most powerful country in the world, Trump became like a casino owner/mob boss who held a monopoly on Vegas. This was especially true since he was enabled by "city hall" — aka Republicans in Congress.

On the surface, the Republican leaders' acceptance of Trump has been just as mystifying as his embrace by evangelicals. But remember: Evangelicals make up the largest and most dedicated single bloc of Republican voters. So if they accept Trump, the party establishment has little choice but to remain loyal to him.

Even though that loyalty only goes one way.

Messianic Mobster

When Trump first ran for president in 2016, he repeatedly threatened to bolt the party and run as an independent if he didn't get the nomination. He scoffed at some long-held Republican principles and denigrated his rivals for the nomination, tagging them with nicknames like "Lyin' Ted" Cruz and "Liddle Marco" Rubio.

Not only did they forgive him, they became his staunch defenders, because they knew one thing: Loyalty is required of subjects, not of kings. Of the faithful, not the savior. Trump views himself very much in royal, messianic terms, and so do his most ardent followers — evangelicals, who are used to viewing loyalty in precisely these terms. Humans are "sinners" who continually fall short of God's glory. But God, on the other hand, is under no compulsion to obey his own rules: He can break or alter them as he sees fit, just like a casino owner can, and just the way Trump insists on doing.

It's a simple matter to dismiss the question of why God lets bad things happen to good people. The response? Blame the questioner for having the audacity to ask about it in the first place.

God is nothing if not mysterious, beyond the ability of man to comprehend. Mystery is essential to faith, which is needed to fuel dopamine and, thus, loyalty. Trump may not be too smart about a lot of things, but he understands this principle every bit as well as any televangelist, and has been able to translate it into the realm of politics.

Trump perpetuates mystery by answering questions about his plans with pat or vague responses. Something will happen in "maybe two weeks" or, more generally still, "we'll see." On one level, Trump may simply not know the answer to such questions. But his genius is that he's able to keep people guessing — and in so doing, keep the focus on him. He's the gatekeeper: the one person who *can* answer the question, even if he *chooses* not to.

When he invokes the "two weeks" timeline, it's just a placeholder. Typically, the time passes, and nothing materializes. It's happened when he's referred to that timeframe in promising new initiatives on infrastructure and health care, among other things.

So why isn't he held to account?

Again, the answer lies in the evangelical mindset: Faith isn't just the assurance that something *will* happen, but the certainty that *it already has.* If God has said it, you can count on the fact that it's woven into the fabric of eternity, because time is meaningless to God.

If your senses tell you something different, the problem is your perception. God is not obligated to explain himself, but you're obliged to believe. To have faith.

"For who has known the mind of God? And who has been his advisor?"

It's a rhetorical question asked first in the

Old Testament writings of Isaiah, then paraphrased by the Apostle Paul in his seminal letter to the Romans. It's pretty much a catch-all rejoinder that excuses God from any charge of cruelty or injustice, because he's above it all.

Trump has repeatedly cast himself in similar terms, refusing to listen to advisors because he insists he knows more than they do. His supporters believe him because his behavior is so familiar, mirroring that of God in the Bible: beyond understanding, yet also beyond reproach. And since they see him as God's chosen vessel on Earth, his unpredictable behavior only binds them more closely to them.

If he tells them something, it must be true, regardless of what their own eyes might tell them.

Faith demands it.

They need faith to maintain the dopamine-driven high of their own expectations. Trump has subscribed to this philosophy himself since his youth, when his father indoctrinated him in

Norman Vincent Peale's "The Power of Positive Thinking." The similarities to the prosperity gospel are striking.

Harnessing Superstition

Psychologists call it magical thinking, the idea that there's a causal relationship between two unconnected events. Another word for it: superstition. If you step on a crack, you won't break your mother's back. If you find a penny and pick it up, it doesn't guarantee that "all day long you'll have good luck." Just because something rhymes doesn't make it so.

Lighting a green candle won't bring a financial windfall, and lighting a red one won't bring love. People typically poo-poo such ideas as childish, but if they're couched in Christian terms, they can seem more credible. "Name it and claim it" isn't any different than lighting a candle; just because you want something doesn't mean it will happen. You can help make it more likely to happen by taking action related to your goal: If you want a job, you have to be qualified, and you've got to apply. That's the old-school Republican concept of personal responsibility. But increasingly, since the party allied itself with the evangelical movement, it's been replaced by the conviction that you can make things happen through wishful thinking.

Trump didn't fit with the old-style GOP. He didn't succeed through hard work, but by using smoke and mirrors to game the system. He took shortcuts and managed to make them work, giving hope to others who thought it would be great to emulate him.

He exploited that desire by opening Trump University, a real estate program that promised students they could replicate his success. Of course, they didn't, and an article in the conservative National Review labeled the whole thing a "massive scam."

The school went out of business, frustrated students took legal action, and Trump wound up settling three lawsuits for a total of $25 million.

But by this time, however, the gospel of wishful thinking had become so ingrained in the Republican Party that it didn't matter.

"When victimhood is your empowerment, recovery is the enemy."

Tammy Bruce,
conservative commentator

Out with a Whimper

Donald Trump lost in 2020.

He tried to deny it. He tried to overturn it. He tried to obstruct the transition. But the truth is that some 80 million people voted for Joe Biden — and against him, the highest total in history. But more than 73 million people voted *for* him, too.

Not all white evangelicals voted for Trump, but the vast majority of them did. And they weren't the only ones to vote for him, either any more than they were the only ones who voted for Ronald Reagan. Plenty of other people did, too, for a variety of reasons.

Trump consistently polled well on the economy, and that was undoubtedly why a lot of people outside his "base" voted for him. They'll move on to someone else soon enough when he's gone, just as they moved on to him from earlier champions like George W. Bush, Mitt Romney, and Paul Ryan.

It isn't about Trump at all for them, it's about what he can do for them. But when it comes right down to it, that's what it's about for his base, too.

The sad truth about Trump is that nobody really loves him, not even his base. They don't even like him, they put up with him, and he's got no one to blame but himself.

For all his marketing genius, he never actually sold Donald Trump to his followers. Instead, he sold them on what he could do for them. His relationships with them were purely transactional, which is exactly what we should have expected. He's never had relationships in the traditional sense; instead, he's just made deals.

His closest "relationships" aren't expressed not in hugs and warm smiles (he doesn't even like handshakes), but in payoffs and nondisclosure agreements. His inner circle consists of sycophants, lawyers, and conservative pundits. He's attracted to models and beauty queens and, apparently, to porn stars. His biggest supporters are white evangelicals who want to rule the world and wealthy businessmen who want to avoid paying taxes.

They understand each other. He uses them, and they use him. It's a marriage of convenience, and an abusive one, as well. Is it any surprise that the same man who bragged about kissing and groping women without permission assaults those who leave or cross him?

With that kind of approach, it's easy to understand why no one likes him. One-way loyalty isn't friendship.

It's exploitation.

But loyalty really does work both ways, and

Trump knows it. That's why he's such a sore loser: because, if he loses, he's got nothing left. All that binds his followers to him is his ability to give them something they want — either by "winning" or by validating their grievances — and to threaten them when he can't.

That's why he couldn't admit he lost the election. If he had, he'd have lost the only thing keeping his base loyal. Without "winning," he'd no longer have them. And without them, he'd have nothing. He'd be alone.

His Worst Nightmare

It's common knowledge that people who are bullied don't love those who torment them. Quite the opposite. But what isn't so widely known is that the people who enable bullies don't love them, either. They use them for protection or intimidation, but love them? No, it's all about what the bullies can do for them, not about who they are.

JESUS, YOU'RE FIRED!

Bullies don't have to have character. They just have to perform, and that's all Trump has ever done. He's pretended to be his own PR man, played "the boss" on TV, and played at being president. All the world's a stage for him, and like any self-absorbed performer, he's obsessed with ratings and can't stomach bad reviews. Worse still, he can't take it if his show gets canceled.

Now, Trump's presidency's been canceled, and he can't take it.

If he can't control the levers of power anymore, he knows his opponents will mock him and ultimately dismiss you. But that's not what really scares him. He's made his peace with that. What he fears most is the prospect that his base will dismiss him, too. That he'll become the butt of *their* jokes. Because, when he can no longer deliver by "winning" or stoking their fears, they'll have no more use for him.

Trump lost in 2020. Not heroically like John McCain the POW or gracefully like

243

McCain the presidential candidate. No wonder he hated the man so much. He had something Trump threw away a long time ago: real love and true respect.

Now Trump has lost, too, but he has neither.

So, who's the real loser?

"The end justifies the means.
But what if there never is an
end? All we have is means."

Ursula K. LeGuin,
The Lathe of Heaven: A Novel, 1983

The End...

Repeat after me: The end justifies the means. If you ever find yourself scratching your head when a white evangelical Christian appears to brazenly contradict his own principles, refer back and repeat again.

It's all you need to know.

The phrase sums up the philosophy of Niccolò Machiavelli, whose brand of ruthless politics earned him fame, or, rather, infamy, in the Middle Ages. The upshot is that actions aren't morally right or wrong in and of themselves; their morality is determined by their results —

which leads to the conclusion that might makes right.

If you've ever wondered why evangelical faiths, which preach things like turning the other cheek and practicing unconditional love, resorted to crusades and violent jihads in the service of that "love" ... refer back and repeat again. This was their mindset. It had nothing to do with love, and it was anything but unconditional. Believe or die. It was as simple as that.

Why do people who profess to believe in honesty, compassion, respect and fidelity support a pathological liar who brands refugees as rapists and brags about grabbing women's genitals without permission? Refer back and repeat: The end justifies the means.

Whenever your first moral imperative is evangelism — to convert others to your way of thinking — all other principles are open to compromise. Even such lofty principles as unconditional love. Instead of offering such love freely, evangelicals too often resort to placing conditions on receiving it (at which point it's no longer unconditional at all).

In the Middle Ages, the only thing unconditional was your surrender. The terms were dictated at the point of a sword, as in the crusades, or on the threat of being burned at the stake, as in the Salem witch trials — where the "choice" was really no choice at all. The sinner accused of witchcraft could either refuse to recant and be burned alive, or confess to something they didn't do... and be burned alive anyway.

Their only reward for lying — breaking one of the Ten Commandments — under duress was the promise of heaven from someone about to kill them. Such cruelty by a servant of "heaven" could hardly have reassured them about what lay in store there.

(One caveat: Not all people accused of witchcraft in such situations were burned. Some were drowned. Or crushed to death.)

These days, the methods are seldom physical torture, and the conditions aren't always dictated "on pain of death." But the same principle applies: A quid pro quo is still offered in place of unconditional love, because the ultimate goal of evangelism isn't love, it's conversion. "Love," like torture, is just a means to an end.

The fundamental quid pro quo, for any unbeliever (not just one accused of witchcraft), is the promise of heaven in exchange for a confession of belief. You can make a "deal with the devil," but you also must make a deal with God. Deals — especially when signed under duress — are not unconditional love. But because this particular deal is at the heart of evangelism, it's become a model for evangelicals, who often place conditions on other actions of "love" toward the sinner. They won't scratch your back unless you scratch theirs.

Faith becomes transactional, just like everything in Trump's world.

Not all evangelicals behave this way. Some view love, not conversion, as their prime directive and really do *show* that love without any ulterior motive. But the fact that conversion is the ultimate goal for so many means that "the art of the deal" will always be a temptation for many evangelicals — and one they have a hard time resisting.

Because morality is of secondary importance to salvation, it becomes disposable. And, as a result, evangelicals wind up engaging in something they regularly criticize when others do it: "situational ethics."

For people who profess to believe in absolute principles, this kind of thinking is anathema. Evangelical voices often rail against it. Yet even situational ethics can be excused in the service of evangelism, and the resulting hypocrisy is also permitted if the outcome is a "saved soul."

"When you do it, it's evil; when we do the same thing, it's noble." Because the results are different.

The end justifies the means.

Just Win, Baby

An evangelical's quid pro quo can be as radical as a conversion at gunpoint, or it can be as simple as offering someone a helping hand and "inviting" them to attend church. An invitation like this leaves room for the would-be guest to decline, but it's clear that he's expected to attend. There's significant social pressure to do so under the rule of reciprocity. When someone does you a favor, you feel obligated to reciprocate. The reason is simple: You don't want to remain in that person's debt. The rule of reciprocity gives him leverage in dictating how you discharge that debt, and a suggestion that you attend church can be a way of employing that leverage.

Evangelism is, at its core, convincing (or coercing) someone to believe what you believe. In short: winning. "God" must win, and "Satan" must lose. But the minute you sacrifice principles on the altar of success, you also render labels like "God" and "Satan" meaningless. Undefined by any moral compass, they mean whatever you want them to mean in the moment.

Evangelicals, politically speaking, are often motivated by the stands they've taken on issues such as abortion, same-sex marriage, gun rights, school prayer, and so forth. But even these principles can be compromised or sacrificed altogether in exchange for the overarching goal of simply winning. The idea is that, once they've won, they'll have unchecked power to impose their views on these issues. Power supplants principle as the immediate goal, and the drive to achieve it by winning becomes not only everything, but the only thing.

This is why so many evangelicals who appear to be at odds with Donald Trump on issues of substance and character, support him enthusiastically. They view him as their King David: their champion, destined to win. And if winning is everything, they have everything in common. It's not about love. It's all about the art of the deal: getting the other party to sign a contract that's favorable to your side, even if it means concealing the fine print or forcing a signature under duress. The methods don't matter.

Refer back and repeat after me....

References

"2013 Heavy Hundred," talkers.com

"A Dozen Major Groups Helped Drive the Religious Right's Anti-Gay Crusade," Southern Poverty Law Center, splcenter.org, April 25, 2005

Abdelfatah, Rund. "'Throughline' Traces Evangelicals' History On The Abortion Issue," npr.org, June 20, 2019

Balmer, Randall. "The Real Origins of the Religious Right," politico.com, May 27, 2014

Barnett, Gerald. "Compel them to come in," researchenterprise.org, April 28, 2016

Bastian, Daniel. "When Faith Healers Are Exposed," waivingentropy.com, March 29, 2016.

Belludi, Nagesh. "Group Polarization: Like-Mindedness is Dangerous, Especially with Social Media," rightattitudes.com, Aug. 15, 2017

Blumenthal, Max. "Agent of Intolerance," The Nation, thenation.com, May 28, 2007

Boston, Rob. "It's Official: Jerry Falwell Jr. Has Substituted Donald Trump For Jesus Christ," Wall of Separation Blog, au.org, Jan. 4, 2019

Bremer, Jade. "Michigan Sheriff Urged to Resign over Militia Ties Following Foiled Gov. Whitmer Kidnap Plot," Newsweek, newsweek.com, Oct. 12, 2020

"Buzz interview 1972," The Words of Larry Norman, fehrion.com

Carey, Jesse. "6 Christian Amusement Park And Crazy Attractions That Have Actually Existed," relevantmagazine.com, July 6, 2016

Caralle, Katelyn. "Trump tells suburban women, 'I'm getting your husbands back to work' as he pleads for votes from key demographic, saying 'you better love me," dailymail.co.uk, Oct. 28, 2020

"Deaths Due to Use of Lethal Force by Law Enforcement," ncbi.nlm.nih.gov, Aug. 7, 2018

Edgar, William. "The Passing of R.J. Rushdoony," First Things, firstthings.com, Jan. 2007

"Evangelism and Politics," The American Historian, oah.org

"Field Listing: Government Type," The World Factbook, cia.gov.

Fielder, Tom. "Family split over son's support for Trump," Charlotte Observer, charlotteobserver.com, Nov. 12, 2020

Freisleben, Shayna. "White evangelical support for Trump goes beyond his policies, supporters and historians say," cbsnews.com, Nov. 2, 2020

Frey, William H. "Exit polls show both familiar and new voting blocs sealed Biden's win," Brookings, brookings.edu, Nov. 12, 2020

Geier, Thom. "Jerry Falwell Jr Defends Trump: 'He Does Not Have a Racist Bone in His Body' (Video)," thewrap.com, Aug. 20, 2017

Gatty, Bob. "The Future of the Country is at Stake," notfakenews.biz, Nov. 17, 2020

German, Michael. "White Supremacist Links to Law Enforcement Are an Urgent Concern," brennancenter.org, Sept. 1, 2020

Gerstein, Josh. "Trump campaign deploys Giuliani to assist flailing legal effort," politico.com, Nov. 17, 2020

Gramlich, John. "What the 2020 electorate looks like by party, race, ethnicity, age, education and religion," Pew Research Center, pewresearch.org, Oct. 26, 2020

"Ingroup bias," psychology.wikia.org.

Jackson, Brooks. "Blacks and the Democratic Party," factcheck.org, April 18, 2008

"Jimmy Swaggart Net Worth," celebritynetworth.com, 2020

Jones, Robert P. "White Christian America ended in the 2010s," nbcnews.com, Dec. 27, 2019

Kirby, Jen. "Read: Brett Kavanaugh's angry, emotional opening statement," vox.com, Sept. 27, 2018

Ley, David J. "The Culture of Victimhood," Psychology Today, psychologytoday.com, June 28, 2014

Maglio, Tony and Nakamura, Reid. "115 Cable Channels Ranked by 2019 Viewership," The Wrap, thewrap.com, Dec. 30, 2019

Masci, David. "American religious groups vary widely in their views of abortion," Pew Research Center, pewresearch.org, Jan. 22, 2018

McDermott, Jackie. "School Choice and Separation of Church and State," constitutioncenter.org, Jan. 29, 2020

"Moral Majority Leader, As Quoted In Penthouse, Blasts 'Lust' Story," Sarasota Herald-Tribune, p. 8-A, Jan. 30, 1981

Nelson, Megan T. "The Changing Values of American Evangelicals in Politics," University of Vermont, scholarworks.uvm.edu, 2019

"New Music Interview 1980 Part 1," The Words of Larry Norman, fehrion.com

Newport, Frank. "Religious Group Voting and the 2020 Election," Gallup, news.gallup.com, Nov. 13, 2020

Ostling, Richard N. "Jim Bakker's Crumbling World," Time, web.archive.org, Dec. 19, 1988

Pierce, Jeremy. "Dominionismists," First Things, firstthings.com, Aug. 14, 2011

"Religious Landscape Study," Pew Research Center, pewforum.org

Rex, Amy Harris. "U.S. election 2020: Vote was cleanest in history, cybersecurity chief tells Trump," The Times, thetimes.co.uk, Nov. 14, 2020

Rock, David. "(Not So Great) Expectations," Psychology Today,
        psychologytoday.com, Nov. 23, 2009

Rosentiel, Tom. "Rev. Falwell's Moral Majority: Mission Accomplished?" Pew
        Research Center, pewresearch.org, May 17, 2007

"Rush Limbaugh, a racist? Naaaaah," Hello Dolly Llama,
        hellodollyllama.blogspot.com, Oct. 15, 2009

"The social transmission of overconfidence," American Psychological Association,
        psycnet.apa.org

Schwartz, Matthew S. "Missouri Sues Televangelist Jim Bakker For Selling Fake
        Coronavirus Cure," npr.org, March 11, 2020

Shimron, Yonat. "Poll: White evangelicals are religious outliers on every issue of
        concern to voters, Religious News Service, religionnews.com,
        Oct. 19, 2020

Smith, Tovia. "'Dude, I'm Done': When Politics Tears Families And Friendships
        Apart," npr.org, Oct. 27, 2020

Stevenson, Chris. "'I would like you to do us a favor though': The one sentence
        that could bring Trump down," The Independent, independent.co.uk,
        Sept. 26, 2019

Stuart, Tessa. "A Timeline of Donald Trump's Creepiness While He Owned Miss
        Universe," Rolling Stone, rollingstone.com, Oct. 12, 2016

Tensley, Brandon. "The dark subtext of Trump's 'good genes' compliment,"
        cnn.com, Sept. 22, 2020

"Top 15 Richest and most Successful Pastors In the World," etinside.com,
        Aug. 30, 2020

"Trump's timeline? Always 'two weeks'," axios.com, June 6, 2017

Tuttle, Ian. "Yes, Trump University Was a Massive Scam," National Review,
        nationalreview.com, Feb. 26, 2016

United States Census Bureau, census.gov

Vallejo, Justin. "'Swaths of country believe Democratic Party a front for a
        paedophile ring': Obama rails against tech and right-wing media,"
        The Independent, independent.co.uk, Nov. 17, 2020

Walsh, John. "11 insults Trump has hurled at women," Business Insider,
        businessinsider.com, Oct. 17, 2018

Weaver, Courtney. "Why US evangelicals are flocking to Trump," ft.com,
        Oct. 2, 2020

"White Supremacist Infiltration of Law Enforcement," s3.documentcloud.org,
        Oct. 17, 2006

"Why a $45 Trump prayer coin is no joke," Religious News Service,
        religionnews.com, May 17, 2019

Zirpoli, Tom. "Zirpoli: For too many, concern for the unborn ends at birth," baltimoresun.com, July 3, 2019

About the author

During a 30-year career in journalism, Stephen H. Provost worked as a managing editor, copy desk chief, columnist and reporter at five newspapers. Now a full-time author, he has written on such diverse topics as American highways, dragons, mutant superheroes, mythic archetypes, language, department stores and his hometown. He spent a decade attending evangelical churches and has written extensively on the subjects of spirituality and religious history. He's also the author of "**Political Psychosis**," an analysis of Trump's political strategy, and "**Media Meltdown: In the Age of Trump**," which examines Donald Trump's relationship with the news media. Read his blogs and keep up with his activities at stephenhprovost.com.